a guide to

recognizing your saints

recognizing

a guide to
your saints

by dito

**with photographs by
Allen Ginsberg and Bruce Weber**

thunder's mouth press • new york

Published by
Thunder's Mouth Press
An Imprint of Avalon Publishing Group Incorporated
161 William Street, 16th Floor
New York, NY 10038

Library of Congress Cataloging-in-Publication Data:

Montiel, Dito.
    A guide to recognizing your saints : a memoir / Dito Montiel.
        p.cm.
    ISBN 1-56025-474-2
        1. Montiel, Dito. 2. Models (Persons)—United States—Biography.
        3. Musicians—United States—Biography. 4. Gutterboy (Musical group)
        5. Authors, American—Biography. 6. New York (N.Y.)—Biography.
        I. Title.

CT275.M58417   A3   2003
974.7'1043'092—dc21
[B]

                                                                2002075073

          9   8   7   6   5   4   3   2   1

Designed by Kathleen Lake, Neuwirth and Associates, Inc.
Printed in the United States of America
Distributed by Publishers Group West

CONTENTS

healing

And God saw the light, that it was good.

Gen. 1:4

a guide to

recognizing your saints

growing up
under the rr

FATHER ANGELO
PEZULLO

when I was a kid there was this priest in my neighborhood at the Immaculate Conception Church in Astoria,
Queens, named Father Angelo Pezullo. There was something
about the way he'd look at you, the way he'd talk to you, the
way he'd smack you in the head when you did something bad
that made you believe him, made you know he was for real.

On Sunday mornings I can remember all of us getting
together at the Immaculate Conception Church on Ditmars
Boulevard and 29th Street. It would usually be me, Giuseppi,
Antonio, Graziano, and sometimes even the Emanuel brothers.
We'd all stand in the back of the eleven o'clock mass making

animal noises and playing tackle football in the Saint Anthony shrine with folded-up church pamphlets whose only other purpose, if folded correctly, was to be shoved down the twenty-five-cent holes of the electric novena candles, getting them to light up, saving a quarter, and getting a free prayer at the same time. The Saint Anthony shrine was our little hideout just out of the sight of the church ushers, better known as off-duty baseball coaches for the church's Little League teams, bouncers for God, scrip lottery football sheet pick'em salesmen, and realistic penance enforcers for the restless and unmanageable noise-makers in the back (they could kick serious ass).

I can still remember Mr. Pugliaci, deaf as a doornail, telling us so loudly to keep quiet that the entire church would turn around. Or the always congested Mr. Marigaliano coughing up buckets upon buckets of phlegm, screaming out his unbelievable grammatically incorrect bilingual curses while still somehow managing to chase us down 31st Street with his long blessed money holder.

Then there was Thursday night confession. Now there are two kinds of people that go to confession. The kids who are committing all the sins and lying through their teeth about them, and the army of old Italian ladies all dressed in black repenting for all the kids who are sinning and lying.

So if you were Catholic and a kid at our church this is how confession would go. First you and all the other kids in the neighborhood would get in what was probably the most informal and easiest line to cut you had ever seen. On your journey from the back of that line to the front, I'm not sure exactly if or where it was written but I believe that everything from wrestling to *delehantes* (the twisting of the arms) to the infamous two-armed Bruno Samartino full-nelson headlock thrust was not only permitted, but mandatory. You would then move on to lie swapping. Now the secret of a truly successful confessional lie would be not to go overboard sounding too good, but also not to repeat any of the same ones the other guys on the line were using. What you had to come up with before you got to the front was a sin you felt was comparable to yours so that you would get the correct amount of penance, but respectable enough to tell your priest. So say you stole ten dollars from the poor box at the church, you might say you stole some candy bars from Genovese Drug Store and also cursed your mother. And before you knew it, before you could even remember your act of contrition or come up with that perfect confession, there you were, next. And if you were next at the Immaculate Conception in Astoria, your prayers had now changed from the need for a good memory or a good lie to the hope that whoever was in Father Lyons's booth was one hell of a long confessor and whoever was in Father Angelo's booth was almost done.

Father Lyons, with his full head of grayish white hair and bluest Irish eyes, we not only believed could see through that supposedly impenetrable partition, but clear through to our very souls. And as if that weren't enough, following your confession, he'd sometimes even throw your name in after his deep bellowing baritone "Amen," causing near-coronaries among the entire sixth grade. On this Thursday, though, we'll say you got lucky and ended up in Father Angelo's booth. "Father forgive me for I have sinned, it's been a while but you know those candy bars looked good, and I was hungry . . . and then my mother was yelling." He'd look back over at you, and he knew. Everybody knew. I mean who were we fooling? How many candy bars could we possibly say we were taking? We were running the entire neighborhood and some of us weren't even teenagers yet. The Greeks on 37th Street had us ripping off the Italians on 29th Street, the Italians had us doing it right back to the Greeks, and you could always get a quick fifty bucks for burning down any of the Hindu newsstands whether they did something or not (the Greeks loved that). But Father Angelo, he knew, and he'd show us he knew by hitting us up pretty hard with that penance. I mean, whoever heard of fifty Hail Marys for a stolen Baby Ruth bar? But you felt better anyway because Father Angelo knew.

After finally finishing at least half a dozen half-forgotten Hail Marys and Our Fathers, I can remember every once in a while kneeling to Saint Anthony in moments of almost enlightenment and wondering how many it would take to truly be forgiven.

The other day I went by the Immaculate Confession, sorry, Conception Church. It's been a while. I walked by the front entrance where Father Angelo would always stand after mass kidding around, grabbing babies' cheeks, smacking wise guys' heads. I thought of old Father Lyons and his endless quest year after year to find out who had stolen the baby Jesus out of the Nativity scene in front of the church. I looked inside. It seemed so much smaller. So much quieter now. St. Anthony's shrine still the same, beautiful and proud. Same electric candles. And then there it was, just to the side of aisle 34, our old confessional booth. Majestic, still tall, less intimidating though, and it was at that moment Father Angelo Pezullo came to mind. All the good thoughts of him. And it was then that I realized him to be my first recognized saint.

ORLANDO
MONTIEL, SR.

then there was my father. Born in 1919 in Nicaragua. He came to New York in the early twenties and never left except for one brief trip to Chicago for the 1939 Golden Gloves. In 1938 he won a diamond belt in a local New York amateur boxing competition and hocked it a week later to buy a wedding ring for my mother.

My father, who has lived through the entire careers of Humphrey Bogart, James Cagney, Marilyn Monroe, Elvis Presley, Frank Sinatra, and The Beatles, has somehow achieved the unbelievable by not only not acknowledging their existence, but by truly not even knowing who they were. Outside of the songs

"My Wild Irish Rose," "La Paloma," and various hymns, marches, and anthems (preferably "The Halls of Montezuma"), there is no specific music. Just music as a general thing. As, in his words, "That's music, right?" Not sarcastically. Just general. Like as to say, "More vegetables?" Not more carrots or peas. Just vegetables. Music. Not opera. Not rock 'n' roll. Music, general. Yes, I like music, but is this good?

My father is not one to reminisce. He tells four stories of being a kid, which consist of:

1. Him lending the boxer Sugar Ray Robinson a dollar in 1939 and never letting him pay it back so that he could always say Sugar Ray owed it to him.

2. He and his friends Jimmy Foy and Rocky Biscaglia swimming across the Hudson River from where they lived in Spanish Harlem to New Jersey and back (splashing rats so they wouldn't get bit).

3. The horses that used to pull the vegetable stands around in Manhattan dying and being left in the streets for days, and how he and his friends would have competitions to see who could pull the dead horses' bodies the farthest.

And 4. Which, like the others, unfortunately until now has never truly been documented in text, the infamous story of his first girlfriend, Mary No-Nose, whom he swears to this day had no nose, and her mother didn't either, and No-Nose was truly their last name.

Like many other kids in places like Queens, one of my fondest memories of my father unfortunately involves an accordion. I had been taking lessons for about three years from a friend of his named Mr. Frank. Mr. Frank was from Sicily, and aside from a few various broken-English obscenities almost always followed by hysterical fits of laughter, he told only one story which, after three years of repeatedly hearing, I had finally made out to be something about him eating the index finger off of "a wild man," in his words, *uno pazzo!*

After my very interesting three-year relationship with Mr. Frank, my father finally figured that I had probably taken enough accordion lessons. Mr. Frank had just been arrested for the third time by the ASPCA for eating half the neighborhood pigeons. My father didn't exactly condemn him for this, but by the third offense, it was strange enough behavior that he had me call it quits with the accordion.

I had already learned "The Star Spangled Banner," along with at least three other countries' national anthems, and I mean where do you go from there?

My father and his friend Bobby Valenti (the cabbie) on finding out about the ASPCA incident:

> **Bobby Valenti:** Orlando, what happened over there with the accordion guy Frank, I hear he's been eating some pigeons or something like that, what's he, crazy!?
>
> **Father:** Nah, it's no big deal, the guy's from Italy, comes here trying to make a living and sees a bunch of pigeons flying around which would be the same thing as if you were in a new country and a bunch of wild chickens were flying all around. So he cooks a few up, what are you gonna do? The guy was hungry I guess.

After the unfortunate decline of Mr. Frank my father was still so proud of my playing that at least once a week he would take me and my accordion with him when he headed uptown to work as a typewriter mechanic on 125th Street and Lennox Avenue. He'd bring me and my best friend Antonio over to Maxie's pawnshop on Martin Luther King Boulevard and leave us there all day to play music for his friends while he went to work. Antonio was from Naples and would do this crazy little Italian dance called "La Tarantella" to just about anything that I would play. Maxie and Mr. Bernhard would give us free lunch and then we'd perform out front with an open case for the rest of the day to make some money. When my father got out of work at five o'clock he'd come straight down to Maxie's, pick us up, take us to Amsterdam Avenue, and treat us to the most greasy, most delicious Spanish empañadas that you could ever dream of.

Looking back now, the idea of two little seven-year-old white kids, one on the accordion playing "The Halls of Montezuma," the other playing some crazy home-made improvisational version of "La Tarantella" in front of a pawnshop in the middle of Harlem seems pretty insane. But that never crossed my father's mind. We were performing for all of his friends on the great stage of New York, and that made him proud.

Nothing ever seemed to affect him very much. And I mean nothing. I can remember coming home on the coldest days in the middle of the most freezing New York Februarys wrapped in my giant Minnesota Vikings snorkel and saying like anyone else, "Wow, it's cold out there," and without exception, never, and I do mean never, would it fail that from some remote corner of the house would come, "What do you want, it's winter."

And you know, it wasn't like I was looking for him to dwell on it with me. To be honest, it wasn't like I was even saying it to anyone. I was simply doing my part as a member of the human race and following that unwritten law that states that whenever you come in from any extreme climatic condition you must verbally acknowledge it. But my father would always be right there to trigger another long, desperate, drawn-out but hopeless battle for his recognition of the simple existence, at any level, of a climate.

"Daddy, will you please just answer the question. Is it cold outside?" His reply always being, "It's winter." Not "Yes, it's cold but it's winter." Not "Yes, but I expect it to be cold in winter." You see, either of these would have been more than satisfying to me. But his verbally strategic answer would simply be, "It's winter." Acknowledging my frustration he'd then throw, in his very nonchalant way, a:

"Look Dito, is it winter?"
"Yes it is winter," I'd say, "and now will you answer a question for me?"
"Of course," he'd smirk.
"I know it's winter, but isn't it also cold?"

Just as the laws of gravity and nature can and will proceed in the ways in which they do, so it went that my father would start it all over again by answering with that kind of frank half-laugh, "Dito, it's winter."

My mother, much more experienced in the appropriate psychological-warfare tactics for this sort of predicament, would then usually step in.

"Orlando, for God sakes, it's freezing out!" she'd say in her unique uncaring but vigorous Brooklyn way. To his predictable reply she would then give up.

And now, looking back, I sure do miss him bugging me like that.

Aside from the many ridiculous seasonal and climatic arguments (and believe me, no climate was safe: "Dito, it's summer"), there were many times in my life that my father, probably more than anyone else, said or did something that has never left me. One time in particular stands out.

I was fourteen. It was July ninth—Antonio's sixteenth birthday. We had been fighting back and forth with another neighborhood in Woodside for about a year. The last time had been about three weeks earlier and it was the worst yet. We all had our trophies to prove it. My friend Johnny Grudy was in the Astoria General Hospital getting the whole back of his head stitched up. Eugene McQuairy was in the emergency intensive-care unit of Beth Israel on 16th Street in Manhattan with a

11

concussion and two metal rods inside his legs, which he still walks around with. While I somehow got lucky and picked up a dimple, perfectly placed on the right side of my face, by a broken Old English Malt Liquor bottle.

It had gotten pretty rough on both sides. As rough as we were going to let it get. We decided to go back the next week and hit them so hard, so brutal, there would be no more retaliation. That Wednesday night we all got together and drove down across this old bridge that connected our neighborhoods. After about three hours of driving around we finally found them hanging out on the corner of Newtown Road. We circled the area for about twenty minutes making sure that they were all there. At just around midnight we poured out of three vans and two cars like a SWAT terrorist team, armed with bats, chains, and whatever we could get our hands on. They weren't ready. We caught them one by one, up Queens Boulevard, down Newtown Road, and then on 66th Street and Woodhaven Boulevard it happened . . .

We were going at it in front of this candy store on the downtown side of the street. We had two of their main guys down inside a bodega halfway down the block. Their faces were so covered in blood from Johnny's spiked brass knuckles that it looked like he and the other guys were in there pounding on a side of freshly cut roast beef. All of a sudden, from across the street I saw Antonio nail this guy with a bat. It was like I was watching some wild action movie in slow motion. Frame by frame. I mean I don't think I had ever seen anyone hit so hard in my life. I really thought the guy's head was gonna come off. Me and Graziano ran over. There was blood everywhere. Antonio had been whipped across the mouth with a chain and was completely out of his mind out of control. He was standing triumphantly over the guy with both of his arms raised like some victorious 15th-round Jerry Quarry spitting blood everywhere screaming "Yeah, mother fucker, yeah."

The next thing I can remember was running across the Pulaski Bridge. There were about twenty of us. It really felt like we were in a movie. Cop sirens were everywhere. It sounded like there was a four-alarm fire happening in midtown. There were people screaming and from a distance you could see the police lights heading our way. I can remember feeling excited and terrified all at the same time. For a moment I thought about jumping down three stories off the bridge but there were even cops down there. We kept running, and all of a sudden, like some Lone Ranger or a last-minute rescue plane in a James Bond movie, our friend Nerf came flying up behind us, beeping his big brown noisy Nova. About eight of us piled in and flew straight back to one of our regular hangouts in Astoria, Perry's Delight.

When we arrived, Perry's was closing up but the owner, Bob, let us in so that we could wash up and talk in peace for a while. Bob was always cool to us. We used to steal him cartons of cigarettes, cheap watches, and batteries from the Woolworth's down the block. Usually when we'd go back to Perry's after a fight we'd end up sittin' around bragging to the girls, laughing, ripping off the pinball machines, eating Bob and Charlie's late-night pizza with extra cheese, sipping plain slushes, and forgetting all about it. But this time we knew it was going to be different and that there was nothing we could do. Antonio, cool as always, reassured us it was no big deal.

The next morning we heard that Tony Stubby, Billy Neilston, and Little Tony Mustache had all gotten picked up by the cops. This was bad and we knew that something big was about to go down. That night we all met around nine o'clock at Perry's. I can remember the time because *Happy Days* and *Laverne and Shirley* had just ended. At around nine-thirty, just as we were getting ready to leave, we were surrounded by at least two dozen cops—plainclothes, in uniforms, DTs, man, it looked like they had half the army out there waiting for us.

They drew guns and threw us against the wall. From a blacked-out window someone pointed to Antonio. They took him away, and just like that it was all over. Antonio, who had just turned sixteen, was charged with manslaughter. He was one of the first juveniles in New York history to be tried and convicted as an adult, and was sentenced to six to eighteen years in prison. He was denied bail because of rumors that tickets to Naples were waiting for him. And tickets to Naples *were* waiting for him.

I remember visiting him before his sentencing at our local jail, Rikers Island. I'd sneak in a few small hits of purple mescaline that would have us both hysterically laughing about non-sense and escaping for the entire visit. It all seemed so unreal. I mean, we were invincible and the thought of Antonio, of all people, not being able to just walk right out with us was hard to believe at the very least.

Antonio was only two years older than me but always treated me like I was one of his little brothers. Whenever I'd come home late, get into trouble, or do anything, he'd always be sitting right outside with my father waiting for me, asking me where I'd been and just telling me what to do. If anybody messed with me, and I mean anybody, before I could even think of doing anything he'd be all over them. He was a maniac and probably the best friend I ever had.

I met Antonio and his brothers, Giuseppi, Angelo, and Lucio, when we were all around six or seven years old. They were a gang of complete lunatics who had just moved into the neighborhood from Naples. We met at one of the Saturday after-noon matinees in the Immaculate Conception Church and became immediate friends for life. The movie *The Seventh Voyage of Sinbad* was playing when all of a sudden a bottle rocket Giuseppi shot at the screen caught it on fire and all the kids were evacuated. While being evacuated I saw him and Antonio cracking up laughing and thought, "I can be friends with these guys." I taught them English and baseball while they taught me soccer and Italian curses. We ripped off trucks together, played strike box together, fought together . . . did everything together. We became family, blood brothers, and now Antonio was down and I couldn't do anything about it.

On the day of his sentencing I was so sure he was going to get off that I didn't even go to the courthouse. When I came home that afternoon I remember seeing Giuseppi sitting outside my house talking with my father. When I asked them what happened Giuseppi said that his brother was smiling when they took him away. When they told me how much time he got I couldn't believe it. I thought maybe with a decent lawyer instead of a public defender he might at least be able to get a reduced sentence. I went to the Italians on 29th Street asking for help since they were always bragging about how many connections they had. They didn't want anything to do with some kid in trouble. They said that he was crazy and that some time would do him good. As for the Greeks, I mean, they never really cared anyway. I still never thought he would get as heavy a sentence as he did, but when you're poor, white, and don't have any connections, you find out about a whole new prejudice in our system.

15

The way that my father fits into this whole whacked scene comes after the sentencing. Everyone turned their backs on Antonio. No one cared. No one visited him anymore. Our insane warrior hero who never let us down, hooked us up everywhere, treated us to Peepland (the big neon eye on 42nd Street), along with countless other strip joints and backstreet whorehouses as minors on Times Square, was down. Caught, a disgrace, and erased from everyone's thoughts for the very same crime that every single one of us was guilty of. I couldn't understand it.

My father took me aside and told me that Antonio was my friend. He told me that no matter what happened, I should stand by him. Now was when he needed me. I couldn't let him down.

My father didn't condone a lot of the things that we had done as kids, but he loved us—us, me, it didn't matter who. We were all the same. Kids from nowhere going nowhere. He always saw a light through the darkness. Knew the cracks let that light in, and that those same cracks could suck you up. He smelled goodness in the streets and saw angels in beat-up old Salvation Army coats (stolen from the big metal Salvation Army collection boxes). Although he probably wouldn't know what the hell I was talking about if he read this, it truly is the way that he was. Tough, strong, loyal, real. The most real person I've ever known.

ANTONIO

antonio spent six years in jail. The first
year I visited him almost weekly but after he was sent upstate
to Dannemora for the remainder of his sentence we slowly but
surely lost contact with each other. Every once in a while his
name would come up in an old fight story. So many guys
from the neighborhood were up there, I didn't think he'd be
too lonely.

I answered my door six years later to this big wild mustached Antonio. I didn't even recognize him. We shook hands,
hugged each other, and decided to take a walk around the
neighborhood. It was real funny watching him point out how

things had changed because to me it all seemed pretty much the same. We did however have a big laugh at the Café Italia, now called The Greek and Italian Café, since they used to pay us to screw each other.

In celebration of Antonio's release I got all the guys from the neighborhood that were around for some drinks at Mio's bar. Mio was a good friend of ours whom we had all grown up with and trusted entirely. When we were kids we used to sell cases of beer stolen from the feasts to his father's bar on 29th Street, which was now his. Mio's was the only real after-hours place that anybody from the area ever went to. You could show up there at just about any hour and find it packed with everyone from local, well-connected, small-time guys to the older Mafiosos playing poker or some loud Greek card game in the back rooms. Tonight though, Mio's bar was open only to us. Antonio was home and we were there to celebrate. We all got smashed on Fat Louie's homemade mixture of every drink in the house served with a flame on top. One of the only things I even vaguely remember was Nick "The Eye Fresh Squeeze" Futamundo (he had a bad eye and used to sell fresh-squeezed orange juice in Manhattan) up on the roof in his underwear trying to shoot the windows out of the Standard Doll Company two blocks away.

After that night me and Antonio didn't see much of each other. I was twenty now and hung out mainly on the Lower East Side of Manhattan playing music with my band. He stayed back in Astoria and ended up hanging out with all of our old connections, doing the same old things that had put him and half the neighborhood away in the first place.

About a month later Antonio came down to the Lower East Side with the Emanuel brothers to see my band play at CBGB's. The Emanuel brothers were four absolute terrors that we had grown up with. They were completely ruthless and over the years had fought their way to the absolute top of the Greek

Mafia. After the show, the three younger Emanuel brothers, John, Strati, and Nico, went home, leaving me and Antonio alone with Emanuel (yes, Emanuel Emanuel). Emanuel Emanuel is probably about as close to being an animal as a human can get. Of the four brothers, Emanuel is without question the leader. He is the spitting image of Robert DeNiro's Al Capone and just about as brutal as they come. The last time that I saw Emanuel he had just been busted on a big rap by the feds. Another old friend of ours from the neighborhood named Tony "Beard" (the first of us with facial hair) had tipped off the police on him, looking to cop a plea bargain for a weapons-possession charge. Tony Beard was a CI (confidential informer).

Later that week they found over $100,000 in cash along with what the *New York Post* called "enough guns to start a war" in Emanuel's basement. I ran into him at the St. Dimitrios feast along 30th Avenue on the day that his picture had appeared on the cover of all three major New York papers, one with the headline "The Athenian Connection." The only concern he expressed to me that day, other than the fact that they had chosen such a terrible picture of him, was whether or not any of the guns they had confiscated were ones he had used on people.

Anyway, after my show downtown at CBGB's that night, me, Emanuel, and Antonio went to this little bar that I hung out in on Lafayette Street, called 428. When we sat down this girl Nancy came up to me to say hello. Nancy had just about the biggest chest you could imagine. Her hair was long platinum white and she was wearing a bikini that would have turned heads on a nude beach. Emanuel, in his very solemn sincere and always patient tone, asked me to introduce him to her. Our conversation went like this:

Emanuel: You know that girl!?
Me: Yeah.
Emanuel: She always dresses like that?

Me: Pretty much.

Emanuel: Looks like a skank . . . you introduce me to that girl?

Me: Sure.

Emanuel: (As I move to go toward her, grabs my arm and very seriously, with his low raspy voice) She'll fuck me right?! (shaking his head yes very seriously)

Me: (Low laugh) I hope so.

Emanuel: (Still holding my arm, still calm, and still dead serious) I mean (pause two seconds) because if she won't fuck me dressed like that and I waste my time (pause) I mean I'll fucking slap that skank around.

In the past, I'd seen Emanuel and his brothers do some pretty insane things. One example that comes to mind was the time they dragged two guys who had screwed up somehow into Antonio's basement from out in the snow and kicked both their knees in backwards to teach them a lesson. So I knew just how serious Emanuel could be when he talked like this. I told him that I wouldn't introduce him to my friend Nancy under those circumstances. He understood and the night went on.

Conversations like that went on throughout the night. At around 5 A.M. Emanuel finally decided to leave, so me and Antonio went home together. On the drive back over the 59th Street Bridge in his new BMW we talked about all kinds of old crazy kid stuff. We almost fell out of our seats laughing about the look on my father's face whenever he'd come back from Scaturro's Supermarket and ask us (fully aware of our guilt) why all the gallons of milk in the store had no caps on them. The answer lay in a short-lived advertising campaign that gave you a free ticket to see the Mets at Shea Stadium for every ten milk-gallon caps you turned in. After we turned in hundreds of caps a day for box seats the campaign was called off. Halted probably by a worker in the ticket office concerned about a gang of little boys in serious danger of extreme calcium build-up, or countless supermarkets stuck with full but capless gallons of milk.

Antonio remembered everything. He was still sixteen. Only the rest of us had gotten older. He told me he missed our old times—we never really saw each other anymore. I told him I thought he was too smart to get mixed up with all the garbage going on in our neighborhood. Crack was getting big and people were really getting out of control. He was a boxer and he was great. In his five years upstate he was undefeated. I told him he should follow through with it.

At around six in the morning he dropped me off. When I got out of his car to say good-bye he looked up at me for a moment, then looked away and said, "You know, Dito, it's real tough out here after doing all that time. Sometimes I wish I was back inside."

Two weeks later he got busted big time with the Emanuels. They were all over the papers and I knew that he was going to end up taking the rap. On the Friday after he was arrested I came home from playing a show at around 4 A.M. When I checked my answering machine I heard three quick Ditos. "Dito, are you there?" "Dito, are you there?" "Fucking Dito man, are you there!?" Man that sounds just like Antonio, I said to myself. Sure enough, before I could even fall asleep, two detectives were at my door asking when I had last seen or heard from him.

As soon as the news came on the next morning it was confirmed: Antonio had escaped from Rikers Island. No one knew exactly how. Within two days he was caught at his girlfriend Diane's house. This time he was sent directly upstate to Dannemora County Maximum Security Prison, placed in solitary, and allowed no visitors for six months.

The ironic part of this story goes back to when we were kids. You see Antonio had to always beat me at everything. I can remember once hitting a baseball over the schoolyard's second fence and Antonio staying there all night until he beat the third fence. He was always like that. So of course, when a writer named Cherry Vanilla gets me and my band a big write-up on the People Page column of the *New York Daily News,* Antonio has to do better. The next day on page two:

"Antonio Ruggiera escapes Rikers Island."

The next time I saw Antonio was the last time I saw him. I had driven nine hours upstate to the border of Canada with my girl, Lisa Marie, to a party that the photographer Bruce Weber was having on his private island. There were boats, girls, food, famous people everywhere. I asked Brooke Shields if she remembered being in a horse carriage on 49th and Broadway ten years earlier and being harassed by a bunch of vagabond kids. She didn't, so I didn't feel the need to apologize.

At the party someone mentioned that Dannemora was only half an hour away, so the next morning me and my girl went to see Antonio. He was surprised. I told him about Brooke Shields and the party. He told me about a friend of ours named Squeegie who had just died in there of AIDS, and about this recurring dream he was having about crashing through the six-inch-thick steel-enforced unbreakable glass they have in the solitary confinement cell. He told me that my girl was pretty and then we went on as always about the same old fight stories. As always he tried lightening up the situation by telling Lisa about the time me, him, and Giuseppi all lost our virginity together to Firecracker Cathy Korstakavidis by way of the barter system. We gave her two mats of firecrackers and some Roman candles and she gave us head. He joked about how a month after that when I'd had sex with my first real girlfriend, Dianne Honeyman, and upon cumming (thinking right up until then that I was still a virgin) I said to her, "Is that it? I mean I already did that." And she smacked me so hard I got a black eye.

He then told me that he and his girlfriend, Diane, had gotten married in prison so that they could have weekend trailer visits. I had heard that she was already trying to get an annulment from the church and wanted no part of him anymore, but decided not to say anything. After about two hours our visit was up and I had to leave. I must have looked sad because he quickly chirped, "Don't worry Dito, we see each other again." We both knew it would be a long time.

For the first three hours of my drive home I didn't say anything. Interstate 25 had become one great giant movie screen; I stared, glassy-eyed, at boyhood memories. Visions of our three-parts sugar, one-part milk morning drinks brought on a warm kind of reminiscing smile. Thoughts of our old stealing competitions on Steinway Street—the time we all put on football

uniforms and charged out right past the security guards—were right in front of me.

The next thing I remember was Lisa Marie grabbing my hand, "Hey." I looked over at her and turned off the road to a town called Woodstock. It was Tuesday night. We pulled over to this little shack, The Tinker Street Café. They were having open poetry readings. I sat down with her, held her hand, and all of a sudden, bang. It was OK. I mean Antonio, everything, and I wasn't thirteen anymore.

And they shall roar like young lions.
Isa. 5:29

CHERRY VANILLA talks about her new discovery.

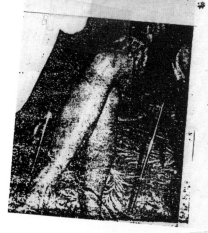

Saturday
A little rock 'n' roll, flavored with Vanilla

The last few times Andy Warhol actress Cherry Vanilla met up with some young musicians, they turned out to be David Bowie, Stewart Copeland and Sting of The Police. So, when the raspy-voiced Ms. Vanilla speaks, we listen. This time, she's gone gonzo over 21-year-old Dito Montiel of Astoria, the lead singer of a group called Gutterboy. They met not too long ago when she did a piece on him for the March issue of Details magazine. "I realized that he was not only cute, but he makes great music as well," said the 44-year-old Cherry. "He's the first new thing to come along in New York in years. So I introduced him to some people." Now, Gutterboy is booked into CBGB's tomorrow and The Saint on the 26th. Okay. What was it like with Bowie, Copeland and Sting? "Bowie was totally unknown in America when I met him in 1971," she rasped. "But he had talent and a sex appeal" that made him "attractive" to both sexes. Copeland and Sting "played backup for me in 1977. I got them their first gigs." And her role with Gutterboy? "Oh," she exclaimed. "I'm their groupie!"

25

Sunday
Rikers escapee nabbed in Queens

By CHRIS OLIVER

An inmate awaiting ▉▉▉ charges escaped from his cell in a protective custody unit at Rikers Island yesterday after leaving a dummy under a blanket in his bunk, officials said.

▉▉▉ Antonio ▉▉▉ 24, a parole violator facing four ▉▉▉ was captured by police 14 hours later in Astoria. It was the second escape from a correction facility in a week.

▉▉▉ used his bunched up clothing to make it appear as if he were sleeping in his bunk.

"He forced open a window in an area outside of his cell," said Corrections Dept. spokesman Tom Antenen.

"The screen was cut and the frame corner was busted, but we don't know what he used to do it. It appears it was done over a period of time."

▉▉▉ later told police he squeezed through bars with Vaseline on his body.

"He scaled a barbed wire fence and cut his hand," said Lt. Thomas Cusanelli of the Astoria Boulevard stationhouse.

▉▉▉ was reported missing at 10:40 a.m. from a protective custody ward at the Anna M. Cross Center on Rikers Island. He was nabbed behind 28-20 34th St. in Astoria at 12:30 a.m. "He started to flee, but one shot was fired by a correction officer," said Cusanelli. No one was injured.

▉▉▉ lived at ▉▉▉ St. in Astoria, before he was arrested and jailed April 10.

Antenen said it is "very likely that there will be disciplinary action against correctional officers.

"Last Saturday, the first escape from the correctional prison barge at the East River on South ▉▉▉ in Manhattan was recorded.

it's about three-thirty in the morning
and I'm at the Times Square station waiting endlessly for my
N train to come take me home. I was about to start writing some
more about Antonio but something just happened that I feel I
have to write down before I don't believe it myself.

About fifteen minutes ago in this exact spot, on a stoop here
at the 41st Street side of the station, I took my book out and
started writing about my saints again. From the tunnel I heard,
"I'll take out this mother fucking razor blade and cut your fucking head off." So I put down my book, put it back in my
Wendy's bag, and went over to check it out.

All of a sudden this insaniac came out of the tunnel and jumped up on the platform. He was completely black with dirt. He walked over to me with the look of 10,000 years of insanity and asked if I minded if he sat next to me. "Sure, as long as you don't ask me for my sunflower seeds." He laughed. When I say he laughed, though, I'm not sure if you know what I mean. He laughed louder than anyone I've ever heard in my life, one of those long hiss kind of asthmatic hysterical laughs that make you crack up as well. "You're all right. My name is Santos," he told me. "You know Santos means saint!" Do you believe he said this? "Santos Antonios, that means Saint Anthony. My mother named me after a saint. The saint of lost articles," he said with a thick proud Spanish accent as I looked at him thinking this was pretty weird. I told him my name and he said he liked it. Of course the feeling was mutual.

He told me he came from the days when pigeons were respected, when "there wasn't a rooftop in New York that didn't have a coop." He then went on to explain how Saint Anthony had earned the title "Patron Saint of Lost Articles." Something about a guy some ten billion years ago losing some "shit" and another guy named Anthony finding it, but being accused of stealing it by the "fucked-up police of ten billion years ago even though the mother fucker was innocent." Santos continued with a detailed, almost first-hand description of the bloody, violent, and untimely endings to both their lives. I offered him some sunflower seeds. "Nah man, that's pigeon food." Walking away he turned back and said, "Now Dito, remember, in life you gotta be crazy." OK, Santos Antonios.

A GAME OF TAG
IN MAYBERRY,
INDIANA

tag was a big deal to me as a kid.

Except for being the year-round third baseman for P.S. 85's concrete schoolyard Hoyt Boys, tag was my thing. Most every night we would meet at Perry's Delight. After hanging out just long enough to empty out all the quarters from the pinball machines with our Fonzie knives we'd walk up Ditmars Boulevard and get the guys in the Greek coffee shops to give us all their stale doughnuts by doing our best Norman Rockwell poor-little-boys-with-fingers-pointing-at-mouths gesturing "we're hungry" through the late-night gate-closing front window. We'd eat some and throw the rest at each other or the

21st Avenue skateboarders. We'd then go by the local Greek and Italian Mafioso hangouts and pick up whatever petty money was owed to us for carrying out some small-time ridiculous job they'd have us do. When we'd leave their downstairs social clubs the temptation to piss through their fanned windows was always there, but then we were talking about at least a good fifteen minutes being chased by Crazy Dimitrios with a meat cleaver. So that was an on-and-off thing. Our favorite money-making scheme by far was cutting the fence with wire cutters and renting out the supermarket's parking lot spaces to people looking for places to park their cars while they went to the neighborhood feasts. On top of the one dollar we'd get for renting the spaces to the car owners, we'd get an additional twenty-five dollars from the towing service for reporting all of the illegally parked cars in the lot.

In summertime it was off to the pool. The biggest city pool in New York was only five blocks away, in Astoria Park. It was about two blocks long. After it would close to the public at 9 P.M., the entire neighborhood would show up, ready for our own party. Since everyone knew the local police and pool workers, no one ever had a hard time getting in at night. The local policemen's duties there included turning the night lights on, kissing some local Mafiosos' kids' asses by handing over loads of fireworks confiscated from the rich kids up in Jackson Heights (their fathers owned cars), and occasionally using the pool's PA system to imitate the theme from the movie *Jaws*. It was a wild place. All of the old Greek and Italian men would be sitting around on beach chairs with their wives, talking, drinking wine, and having barbecues while we'd all be partying and skinny-dipping on the other side. There'd be radios blasting everywhere in the constant never-ending war between rock and disco. Every night someone would make off with an unlucky skinny-dipper's clothes, leaving him to make that long run home without them.

GRAZIANO: Bombs away!

ANTONIO: Yo Graz, you better not be shitting in the water!!

My main reason for even going to the pool was Dianne Honeyman. I was thirteen, and in my eyes no one was as beautiful as Dianne. She'd always be there with her crew of neighborhood girls looking way over-sexy for thirteen-year-olds in their hot pink or purple leg warmers, air-brushed shirts with all their names on them, and perfect red-white-and-blue roach-clip feathered earrings, dancing to songs from the soundtrack to *Stayin' Alive*. But Dianne, man, she drove me nuts. I'd spend just about every minute at that pool begging, trying anything I could to talk her into going to one of our real romantic spots together, like the deserted trash dumps on 21st Street, or any hallway or rooftop we could get on, to try and get whatever it was I could off her. And sometimes I did.

After the pool (or on a good day, the roof) we'd all end up back at Perry's, with the owner yelling because he knew we'd ripped off his machines, his famous line being, "It's a cold winter out there, boys." In other words, you were out for the night. This meant it was time for tag, or "Catch One Catch All." One guy is "it." As he catches people they join him and this continues on until everyone is caught. You could go as far as the Neptune Diner in one direction, the garbage mountain in the other, and Perry's was base. Our choosing process made Three Card Monty look legit. It was cheating beyond belief, but consistent cheating. Nobody strong or fast would ever be "it" first, so the game would always start off with either Timmy Riley, Cliffy, or Tony "Needle Dick" being chosen "it."

Side note: Tony "Needle Dick" had a brother named "Helicopter." I once asked Kevin Gordon, who was in charge of giving people nicknames that stuck, why "Needle Dick's" brother's name was "Helicopter." His answer was, "Because he can suck his own dick!" I never really understood that. Anyway, back to tag.

The cheating would then continue throughout the game. One of the first complaints would usually come from someone like Riley, saying that he had trapped Antonio into a corner but had to let him go without tagging him because of death threats. Then Mio would want to quit. If he was lucky enough not to have been chosen "it," being he was so slow, he'd find a good hiding place that, of course, everyone would yell out and throw rocks in the direction of. Giuseppi would always climb the same giant tree on Chinky Hill that no one but him could get to the top of, and just sit there for the duration of the night. If you find Giuseppi's strategy to be no fun, try Jimmy Dimitrios's. His father owned the Neptune Diner, which was within the boundaries of the game, and Dimitrios would hide in the kitchen, where nobody but him and the workers were allowed, and just sit there the whole game.

Tony Thelesinos and Graziano were the militant tag players, camouflaged by leaves and covered with rocks. We used to let them be free just to see how far they would take things. Johnny Grudy, on the other hand, was the opposite. Because he was slower than everyone else and never truly enjoyed the game, he usually used his freedom to go home until the next day.

Then of course there were the fights, dog chases, injuries, and the possibility that some free member of the game had turned to crime. If you heard sirens, you would drop everything, run to Giuseppi's basement, and start another of the many fun game possibilities for the evening. This could mean anything from the ever-popular sport of throwing heavy weights at each other whenever the lights got turned off, to "death" boxing matches, to our very own unique interpretation of darts (a sort of blindman's bluff, or pin the tail on the donkey with, of course, that casualty element). Whenever I think back to all the games we played as kids, what always gives me a good laugh

31

is how in our neighborhood we would take your everyday type of kids' game and throw in an extra little consequence clause that no one else seemed to have.

One weekend, after ages of thinking about it, we finally brought our game of tag over to Central Park in Manhattan. We were all from Queens and although Manhattan was only ten minutes away on the RR train, when you're a kid, it's a major journey.

I can remember that day perfectly. We left for Manhattan at around 8 A.M. About ten of us all hopped the turnstiles at our train stop, Hoyt Avenue, in Queens, just like they did in that movie *The Warriors* (it was a big thing at the time). We ran endlessly through the train, punching the handrails like speed-bags, tackling each other, and finally blazing out at 5th Avenue, Central Park.

Our first stop was at the Plaza Hotel on 59th Street, at the southeast corner of the park. We ran through the entire hotel stealing tips out of the bathrooms, turning the leftover room service on each floor into literally one giant food fight, and grabbing desserts and pieces of cake off golden-looking trays in the Palm Court that Danny Foley swore cost one hundred dollars each. The security guards made a futile effort to catch and throw us out, but who were they fooling? No meat cleavers. No threats of death. This place was great. I mean, we thought Ditmars Boulevard had a lot of places to mess around. Here we had elevators to stop, horse-and-carriages to hitch on, and a place, FAO Schwarz toy store, with free video games, speed cars, and robots everywhere. We must have sent at least twenty robots down the aisles before getting thrown out. Woolworth's would never look the same again. Manhattan felt like a great unopened oyster full of new places to go crazy in.

As soon as we found Central Park, Timmy Riley was immediately declared "it." Having no conception of its size, we made the entire park the boundaries. Timmy didn't catch one person all day. To be honest, fifteen minutes into the game I believe everyone set off on his own personal expedition through this new uncharted land. A few of us found this one spot in the park where toy electric motorboats sped around a water hole that we immediately turned into a swimming pool. When it got dark we found a loose rowboat floating in a lake. Danny Foley swam out to it, as he was the only guy who could swim. He pulled it over to us and it became our great secret exploring pirate ship. Our imaginations were going wild and we were in midtown. At the end of the night I was so in love with Manhattan that I was sure we'd go back every week from then on.

But we never went again and tag resumed in Astoria. I'd be getting a little too romantic if I said that it was never the same after that, but I do believe that somewhere in the back of my mind I knew I had found true love.

I saw a movie recently where the narrator said, "You never have friends like the ones you had when you were a kid."

To this day I've never stopped dreaming about our game of tag.

33

"CLOWNS"

"there are no saints in the news
media." This is something my mother would say at least two or
three times a week. But each night at 10 P.M. you could always
be sure to find her and my father glued to Channel 5 with news
anchorman John Roland. I know there were much more highly
regarded news anchormen, like Walker Cronkite and Jim
Jensen, but to my father the ten o'clock news with John Roland
was the law.

After long hours of tag and terrorizing the neighborhood I
remember coming home, and at exactly 10 P.M. saying in unison
with my father and the television, "It's 10 P.M.; do you know

where your children are?" Victor Reisel was another of my father's favorites on that news show. Reisel had been blinded by some guy in the mob who threw lye in his eyes. I know this bit of trivia thanks to my father's repetition of this story every night immediately upon Mr. Reisel's appearance.

"Daddy, I know."

"Well, they did."

As my father would put it, the weather guys were always "clowns." So when Channel 9 picked up a nightmare weather caster who would always give long, supposedly funny "hel-looo's" out to the old ladies in New Jersey who would write in requesting them, Channel 9 went off the air at my house. Gimmicks and the news never mixed very well for my father. When an anchorman attempted a gimmick, my father would almost always have the same reaction—a half-laugh, a kind of slow, get-outta-here wave of the hand at the TV. Then he'd say "clowns" as he shut them off while still sort of half-laughing.

John Miller, who joined the Channel 5 news team later on, was another favorite. I believe it was because he had crazy, curly hair but always maintained a serious composure. In an ongoing segment of the news entitled, "John Gotti, The Mafia Don," Miller gained my father's respect forever. "That kid's got guts," my father might comment after watching John Miller chase John Gotti down the street with a microphone and make some sort of smart remark.

Though women were never a hit as news anchors with my father, for some reason Barbara Walters was approved. I think it was because of her groundbreaking salary. "She gets a million dollars," he would quote.

Sports commentators were a strange breed to my father. He loved boxing and all of the New York teams—Yankees, Mets, Jets, Knicks, and Nets—so the commentator could give him the scores and even elaborate mildly on certain goings-on, but if they got a little too carried away with trivia, opinionated commentary, practically any nostalgia, or dared the unthinkable, showing "bloopers," there was always the threat of the plug being pulled and the inevitable "clowns." With news and with sports it was "just the facts."

As I've said before, my father was not one to reminisce or indulge in nostalgia. It was "news for existentialists" or you were off. Once one president was out of office he no longer really existed. Nixon and Ford were never commented on. Watergate was nonexistent. Carter joined that crowd, though Billy Carter on occasion did bring a smile to his face, usually followed by "clowns" and Billy's termination. Reagan was simply, in no positive or negative way, "the actor," and Bush senior never happened.

Though the gimmicks of news anchorpeople were not tolerated, with criminals it was quite the contrary. If you earned a nickname such as "Son of Sam," "The Zodiac," or "Dartman" (though Dartman was so ridiculous his airtime was severely limited), or gained any form of warped recognition, you would at least capture his attention. If you talked to a dog, wore a Spider-Man outfit and climbed the Twin Towers, or parachuted naked into midtown, you would last on our television for the length of your story. But beware, for you were definitely walking that very thin "clowns" line. Only in writing and remembering all this do I realize what a thin line that was.

Then there were the political superheroes like Fidel (gimmick: cigar), Kadafy (gimmick: military attire), Gorbachev (easily identifiable by birthmark on head), and Arafat (for his one comment on how if he were the last Palestinian left with nothing but a sharpened stick he would run at his opposers with it). Though my father didn't agree with most of their policies, these props were always a big hit in our house.

As a kid my many brushes with the news media were as a bystander in the background of either a fire, murder, mob bust, Mets pennant, or as an onlooker at the scene of another Greek Saints bimonthly miracle at the St. Dimitrios Greek Orthodox

Church, which consisted of either crying statues or visions of Irene. All but one of these brushes were uncaptured.

I was sitting and watching the seven o'clock news with my parents when all of a sudden the anchorman said, "And now let's go live to the scene of the murder with David Diaz on 31st Street in Astoria, Queens." Before my mother or father could say anything I was out the door and standing right next to David Diaz live on the news!

Thanks to my dear, now-deceased, quick-thinking Uncle Ernie and his obsession with that new invention "the Betamax," I can be seen to this day in my debut television performance, smiling and waving just to the right of anchorman David Diaz in the background of a bloody murder scene. At almost any of my family's big gatherings this film is still shown among the other home movies, accompanied by my uncle's and aunt's remarks on how good I look on camera. The fact that there is a bloodied corpse no more than three feet away from my adolescent star-struck gleaming attempt for media recognition has never been a factor. As a matter of fact I don't believe it has even been noticed. With this in mind let me quickly run down the order of remarks that will usually accompany the screening, starting with my Cousin Gracie's yearly comment on how everyone on television looks ten pounds heavier than in real life.

> **Aunt Alice's stern yet preoccupied reply:** Yeah, you know that's true.
> **Uncle Johnny's always baffled:** What's that . . . live?
> **Aunt Mary's:** For Chrissakes, Johnny, it's little Orlandito on TV from years ago!
> **Uncle Johnny's laugh:** Well I'll be damned, that is little Orlandito!

In writing about this ritual at my family gatherings one unanswered question eludes me about my Uncle Ernie's involvement in this taping.

My concern is as follows: The Betamax tape that documented this whole event, starring me (the opportunistic onlooker), was left running after David Diaz ended his live telecast on the murder, followed directly by a commercial break. During family gatherings it is at just this time that everyone's attention starts to divert from the set. It's at this moment each year that I'm most captivated. When the news returns from its commercial break, weatherman Dr. Frank Fields (a favorite among the family for his no-nonsense weather), is quite uncharacteristically wearing a bow-and-arrow hat—the kind that the comedian Steve Martin made popular at the time. At that moment, at every showing of that tape, at every gathering of the Nicaraguan side of the Montiel family, out of the corner of my eye I look for my father. Wherever he is standing I can always see him disapprovingly acknowledge the weatherman Dr. Frank Fields' attempt to generate more life in the forecast. I notice that "clowns" look come into his eye, and all I can do is smile to myself because I know from watching this same tape year after year that before he can get from wherever he is standing to that on/off switch, the tape on the Betamax will cut out, going to static, doing the job for him.

The answer to the question why my dear deceased Uncle Ernie, a direct sibling of my father, shut that tape off at that particularly crucial moment must unfortunately remain a secret forever. Coincidence? Could he have called Dr. Frank Fields a "clown?"

saints,
wanderers,
brief
acquaintances

guide to recognizing your saints

WHO IS
LARRY KERT?

when I was twelve years old, my mother took a day off work to bring me to Radio City Music Hall to see the movie *West Side Story*. It was a weekday and some sort of feast of the saint of the great day off from school was taking place. Although I probably would have preferred hanging out with my friends in Hoyt Park playing handball, I was still pretty excited to take the subway into the city.

I spent the entire train ride driving my mother crazy, running back and forth, hopping and spinning around the handrails, and playing this little game I had invented where you kind of closed one eye and flew a stain or dirt spot on your window like an airplane over buildings and telephone poles by moving your head up and down. Until recently when I saw this little black wire-haired kid playing my very same game I thought I was the only one who knew about it.

We started our day off in Chinatown. We always started our days off in Chinatown. She'd take me down to a weird little store on Baxter Street that to this day I've never been able to find on my own. She bought me orange peanut-shaped marshmallows off a bearded Confucius Chinese man who I used to think was 200 years old.

I remember my mother telling me that she loved Chinatown so much because when she was a little girl growing up in Coney Island, Brooklyn, she always thought her father was taking her on a great adventure to some other country whenever he brought her there. I fell in love with it for the same reason.

When we got to Radio City Music Hall I couldn't believe how big it was. My mother bought me popcorn, Snowcaps, and a large Coca-Cola. I knew this was a special occasion as we never had much money, and when she took me to a movie we'd usually sneak in a few cans of C&C Cola and some of her famous spaghetti sandwiches. It was special because Tony was in this movie. You know Tony, the guy who loved Maria. My mother told me that she had been in love with Tony ever since she saw *West Side Story* as a play on Broadway. Over the years the actors playing his part had changed, but she still loved Tony. Tony was strong and brave and handsome and reminded her of my father.

Halfway through the movie I was bored and asking her if we could leave. I wanted to go over to 42nd Street and see a Bruce Lee double feature, especially the one with Chuck Norris and Kareem Abdul-Jabar in it. She assured me that a grand finale fight scene was coming up soon and that I wouldn't be disappointed. Relieved by the news I now sat quiet, impatiently awaiting the big karate showdown between Tony and Bernardo.

The big question was whether Tony would use that great snake move that Bruce Lee had invented, break out some nunchucks, or just go with his own, as-yet-unseen form of kung fu.

My mother, noticing my impatience, told me they were about to go at it. I got all excited. Finally it came. The Jets were heading through this real big schoolyard with Tony right up there leading them. Coming full speed heading right at them was Bernardo's gang, the Sharks. As the moment got closer I became more and more excited. And then, right as they came face to face with each other, right at the peak of their confrontation, just at that moment of truth, what did they do? They STARTED SINGING! SINGING?! I mean these guys would be dead in half a second in my neighborhood. All of a sudden one guy pulled out a knife. I got excited again, but as soon as it turned into some sort of knife ballet I knew *West Side Story* was not for me.

After the fight dance ended I looked over at my mother who was full of tears. I couldn't understand why she was so sad. I mean only one guy had died. In Bruce Lee's movie at least fifty people would have been dead by this point and you'd leave feeling great, but to my mother all that mattered was that Tony and Maria would never be together again and that made her sad.

A few years ago, as many times since then, I was supposed to meet my friend Mike O'Shea on 51st and Broadway. He was driving a cab and was about half an hour late. I thought that he must have picked up some real out-of-the-way fare and probably wasn't going to show up. It was the middle of winter and it was freezing outside. I saw a phone through the big glass doors of the Wintergarden Theater right across the street and decided to wait another fifteen minutes for Mike in their warm hallway pretending to make a call. As I stood there disguised as a phone-talking theatergoer, I began noticing a stream of strange, over-the-top, days-gone-by Broadway actor types walking in. It didn't look like the tourist crowd that you would usually see at a Broadway play. I walked over to one very distinguished-looking overly-made-up older woman and asked her what was going on. She told me that they were having a wake for Larry Kert, who had just died of AIDS. When I asked her who Larry Kert was, she, obviously disappointed by my ignorance, said, "Among many other things Larry Kert was the original Tony in the Broadway version of *West Side Story*." She invited me inside for what she said would be a crash course in New York (say it dramatically) "*theatre!*" With Mike's cab nowhere in sight, I accepted the invitation.

I had never been inside a Broadway playhouse before. It was impressive. They had taken down the set from a play called *Cats* then performing there nightly and had turned the whole place into an old-New-York-looking *West Side Story* stage. There were about fifty of these strange almost-half-familiar older faces all walking around seating themselves. It was like sitting among the uncles and aunts on some daytime soap opera—I'm not sure which one. They were all wearing movie-star-looking outfits with big hats and talking in charismatic dramatic voices. It was all pretty weird.

After about fifteen minutes of low talk and quiet commotion the lights went out and an older man wearing a black and white tuxedo came out on stage to greet everyone. The first thing he said to the small audience was, "My God . . . what happened to you all? You look terrible!" They all started laughing as he explained that that was his best impersonation of a "Larry Kert" greeting. He went on for about twenty minutes about his friend. He told great old stories about the whole gang of them meeting up at the old Howard Johnson's Ice Cream shop on 47th Street after play rehearsals. He talked about trying to pick up Natalie Wood during the intermissions of *West Side Story*, about how Larry Kert used to play jokes on the whole cast on stage, and he reminisced about hanging around being an actor in New York in the 1950s and '60s. After he finished, others came up to tell stories of Broadway and how much fun their lives had all been together. Chita Rivera even came out and danced with no music and the lights real low.

I remember listening to all of their fantastic stories. They were stories about the past, about an era, about a bond they all shared. I felt like I was taking a history lesson for the soul. I was imagining myself hanging with them at backstreet jazz clubs in Tin Pan Alley, late at night on 52nd Street, and going to see locals like Tony Bennett or Duke Ellington play with some girl wearing an old beat-up smoking jacket or cool cool fedora and I couldn't help, of course, but think of how much my mother would have loved to have been at this event.

Their stories were about life and living life. About theater, loving and living it. About success of the heart.

At the end of the night they all seemed so happy. Maybe it was just because they hadn't seen each other in a while, but as they all gathered around hugging, kissing, and well-wishing each other, I found myself feeling for the first time in my life like maybe I'd missed out on something. And I was real glad that I had picked that lobby to get out of the cold and wait for Mike O'Shea in.

JIMMY MULLEN
OF THE BRONX

a half-ridden green diamond-eyed greaser ragamuffin from the Bronx, my closest friend and modern-day saint Jimmy Mullen fell off a Greyhound bus at the 42nd Street depot in New York City after three thousand miles of starvation and withdrawal.

Because he had no suitcase or money, his clothes, all dirty and wet, were completely wrapped up into one giant ball of toilet paper working as some sort of very offbeat, makeshift type of luggage. As he lay all crooked, beat, skinny, and asleep across the center of the bus depot he looked like some junkie with the greatest science project of all time. I woke him up with that half-smiling, surprised, kind of shaking your head "no" look, the kind you give your three-year-old brother when he does something like cover his head with a bowl of spaghetti. After three wake-up shakes and one real loud "JAY!" he finally peeked out and smiled through at least three layers of five-day-old black mascara, and gave a very faint sign of life—a sort of exhausted moaning "Whoa," as in "Whew," as in "man that was some in-fucking-sane trip."

To even attempt to understand Jimmy you'd have to first imagine a half-Irish half-Nicaraguan Keith Richards with a Jerry Lewis voice whose thoughts are wrapped up almost entirely in '70s television and who talks in nothing and I mean nothing but riddles.

Jimmy was born, appropriately, on April Fools' Day in the Bronx but grew up in my neighborhood, Astoria, Queens. In a neighborhood where you didn't show too many feelings, Jimmy's avalanched. He wouldn't think twice about telling you he loved you, even as a kid. In an article I once read about the actor James Woods, the interviewer said that he had never met a person who so badly wanted people to like him. That would be a real good description of Jimmy. Eager to please, real, nothing but good intentions. Add to that one dose of the ingredient "berserk," but really add it. Pour it in.

The first time we met he was introduced to me as "Grease" because of his big, wild '50s pompadour haircut. He greeted me in a rabbit voice and for about twenty minutes talked about Telly Savalas (*Kojak*), Dr. Zachary Smith (*Lost in Space*), then moved on to descriptions of *My Three Sons* episodes that even the original cast could not possibly remember in such detail. All I wanted to do was get the hell away from him. After a while though (and I've seen this happen to almost everyone who has ever met him) he became so much, so gone crazy, that I kind of liked it. I've found only one way of describing this popular reaction to Jimmy's lunacy. It has three stages and it goes like this:

(Stage 1)

Example: You are watching a movie and the guy in it slips on a banana peel.

Reaction: You laugh (it's kind of funny).

Comparison to Jimmy Mullen: First ten minutes of Jimmy talking about *Star Trek* while using alligator voice (it's kind of funny).

(Stage 2)

Example: The guy slips on the banana peel five more times.

Reaction: You are now irritated and not enjoying the movie any longer.

Comparison to Jimmy Mullen: Next hour of Jimmy talking about *Star Trek,* using alligator voice (you are now irritated and not enjoying Jimmy any longer).

(Stage 3)

Example: The guy then proceeds to slip on banana peel one thousand more times.

Reaction: Out of pure disbelief you now begin to enjoy the horribleness of it all.

Comparison to Jimmy Mullen: Fifteen years later, Jimmy still talking about *Star Trek,* using alligator voice (out of pure disbelief you now enjoy the horribleness of it all).

Over the years Jimmy and I became great friends. We made a deal with each other, that if either of us got a job we would get the other guy in. Both of us got fired from the Palladium nightclub for not recognizing and escorting the artist Andy Warhol (who overheard owner Steve Rubell yelling at us, "He's a fucking albino! How could you miss him!?") We went everywhere together—from selling Christmas trees in midtown

Manhattan, to the mind-altering occupation of on-foot city messenger (the only job I truly believe could justify taking hostages), from a short stay at Cedar's Mount Sinai research lab as guinea pigs for insulin testing, to getting fired from Dean & DeLuca's Gourmet Deli by the owner (Giorgio) for going through the garbage late at night on Prince Street looking for all the groceries we had hidden in it.

We'd get high at noon, go back into our hamburger outfits when we were handing out flyers for Arby's, and discuss, sometimes in great detail, how we were living through some sort of long demented episode of the Abbott and Costello television show, then return to harass, to no end, the Arby's baked potato who worked right across from us on the corner of 42nd and 6th. (The potato took his job as seriously as a man wearing a giant sour cream hat could. I think he's still working that corner. Check it out for yourself.) Our endless marijuana-driven confrontations with the baked potato got so bad that one day we took it upon ourselves to attack and tackle him to the ground while in our hamburger outfits. After an order of protection was threatened we decided to move on. Jimmy and I must have had at least twenty jobs together, each one out-bizarring the last.

Between jobs we'd walk from Greenwich Village to Wall Street in delirious matching hot pink Shoo Fly cowboy hats, knickers, leopard-skin vests and giant black patent-leather combat boots, looking like two fag pimps, looking for new jobs. We'd scrape through whatever money we had, get a few slices of pizza at Stromboli's on 1st Avenue and St. Mark's Place and meet up with E.J. (notorious for his long naked run, painted red, through the halls of Geffen Records in Rockefeller Center, throwing his band's demo tapes all over and ending up getting stuck in Barbra Streisand's office); Mike O'Shea (great songwriter, true friend, and cab driver who considers city buses to be: money vacuums, boats on wheels, and government conspiracy vehicles made solely for the purpose of unemploying or

49

"deploying" all hard-working taxi drivers); Nerf (obsessed with knives, extreme mathematical problems, and excessive hair loss); Jimmy Doyle (avid and frequent user of unprescribed Prozac, phenomenal fan of Black Holes, and a self-admitted nonconformable crook after the realization that his bachelor's degree in political science left him qualified for not much other than the dictatorship of a small unmanned country); Frankie Rock (infamous for very seriously and straight-faced coining in his Brooklyn kinda way, this truism: "Ya see once you fuck a chick with any piece of food you gotta be prepared for the repercussions of that action, which are that you will never be able to comfortably order that same food with her again at a restaurant. So use something like an eggplant or something you won't miss too much."). And of course there was Mimi, a little angel Jimmy met and fell in love with at a job we had blowing balloons up all night for a festival on 2nd Avenue.

The three of us would usually meet at a squat down on 6th Street between B and C and walk downtown by the water to what's now called Battery Park City. We'd get high on Old English and cheap wine by this one great area where they had just put these crazy blue lights. The whole place was under construction and was as desolate a place as you could find anywhere in New York. It was beautiful. We'd stay up all night writing songs, roaming around, just wasting time. Some nights me and Jimmy would go there alone with his beat-up old acoustic guitar. I'd watch him play endless songs, all in his head. It was the only time he'd be serious. I remember watching him with nothing but the truest admiration. The words he'd sing were always perfect flawless real beautiful.

Eventually Jimmy and Mimi moved down to this real bad heroin- and crack-ridden block on the Lower East Side, Avenue B and 6th Street, and we didn't hang out as much anymore.

In the next three years Jimmy went from getting high once in a while to doing dope once in a while to sticking so many needles in his arms and legs he could barely walk and sometimes he couldn't walk at all. I'd get hysterical Mimi calls at 3 A.M. from St. Vincent's Hospital on 7th Avenue saying he wasn't going to make it. I'd fly down there in Mike's cab only to find him lying there skinny as a rail, joking like nothing had happened, and then going hysterical crying, telling us how scared he was of dying.

From all the drug abuse, physical abuse, and homelessness he had developed a murmur of the heart, bad asthma, and a cut on his right arm that had led to severe gangrene. I would joke with him about how it wasn't so bad. That if it did get worse and he had to lose his arm I could always sew a cup there, get him a monkey, a harmonica, and a whistle. He'd look over smiling and say with his half-breath, "That's disgusting."

In the last year at least three different times he's tried to kill himself. After his third attempt, his closest to success, we got him on a methadone program, which lasted about a month before he was back down on Avenue D at the laundromat copping dope in drag again as Jenny, since he owed so much money as Jimmy.

As a last resort we all got some money together and bought him a ticket on a Greyhound bus to L.A. so he could clean up at a good friend of ours' place. Before leaving Jimmy gave me half a song and told me to finish it. It was beautiful, just like everything he writes. He said it was about us and it was called "Is It True?"

In L.A. things just got worse. We heard stories from him about demons, from other people that *he* was the demon. He quit his job on Hollywood and Vine working a gay sex phone line (I'm sure that as every television character from Gilligan to Mr. French he was getting people off all over L.A.), and then he disappeared.

For the next two months no one saw or heard from him. Two weeks later I got a call from Amarillo, Texas. It was Jimmy. He was on a Greyhound and would be here in a day, said he missed the subway. I went to the depot the next day and found him a mess. He could barely walk, said he was tired, didn't even have the breath to joke. I took him home and within two days he somehow managed to pick up a girl. They fell immediately madly in love forever and ever and off he was again.

Two days ago I found out through Mimi that Jimmy got some bad blood tests after being arrested and sent to Rikers Island for robbery. I know he was terrified of this. I hope it's not true. He's been calling me nonstop and I don't know what to do. Sometimes I'll just sit there and listen to him yelling on my answering machine in complete desperation. Everyone else has already given up on him. They say at least now he's got a roof over his head and three meals a day. Maybe I'm blind but when I listen to my friend's voice I still hear that crazy sixteen-year-old insane Pied Piper with a pompadour talking like a mad beautiful poet.

Last night at around midnight I took a walk along 6th Avenue with my girl. I told her about how 6th Avenue was one of Jimmy's and my favorite places to go at night. It always seemed so calm and quiet up there after such a crazy day of thousands of workers going to and fro without a moment or a place to rest. I told her how we'd joke about the bums taking it over at night. We stopped behind the great library on 42nd Street to kiss by a new fountain they had just put there. I looked past her shoulder to this one giant star and for one very over-dramatic second thought I saw my friend looking down to me smiling, saying it was all right . . . and it was all right. Maybe that's just how I deal. But that's how I go on. I miss him.

Jimmy taught me to be tougher than the toughest. To be real. To be true. To love. He'd give you what he had. I remember watching him sing like a bird—songs that would make you dream. He said he was always looking for a new color. He used to call me the new color. He said he wouldn't wanna see a spaceship without me. He always talked in riddles, but I think I know what he meant, and I don't think anyone can ever say anything that will mean as much to me.

I love him like a brother. I love him more than a brother. I will always love Jimmy Mullen.

is it true time's gone by but is our love gone too
is it you or have I been sad to find it's never
been you at all
is it true the midnight blue has come to its fair end
is it sad or are you hiding all the love we ever had
                                        —J.M.

travels, deserts, gettin' lost

guide to recognizing your saints

AS FAR BACK AS I CAN REMEMBER... I CAN REMEMBER MANHATTAN

according to a homeless self-proclaimed scholar and ex–lion tamer named Kartun (pronounced Cartoon), who would visit me daily as a kid at my peanut stand on 7th Avenue and used words like col·lo·qui·al [(k-lkw-l)—relating to conversation; conversational], a French poet once said of Manhattan, "Pity the sky with nothing but stars."

And when I pass that undeniable sweet tempting scent of buttered popcorn on the 34th Street platform of the uptown line, I will think about it, but I won't be fooled into buying it, for I know how much better the smell is than the taste.

And please let me warn you about the homeless martian with a Siamese cat on his shoulder, who's probably heading in your direction if an unusually loud and arrogant saxophone sounds like it may be closing in on you through the tunnels of the IRT line (he's gonna ask you for some money to help fix his spaceship).

And is there any true way to put into words the feeling of holding your love on the Delancey Street blue-light docks on a 3 A.M. no-one's-around-Monday-night-but-you? And what could ever explain a springtime 7 P.M. Sunday walk with a good friend down the cobblestones where Prince meets Sullivan Street after a light warm rain and maybe a drink? And you know that proud Spanish strut that just becomes you after eating at Umberto's on that first date and Sinatra's "In The Wee Small Hours of the Morning" just happens to come blaring out of some unexpected third story Mulberry Street window. Or that 47th Street Playland game of Missile Command, hilariously laughing drunk on Old English at 8 P.M. with Michael Alago and Lisa Marie getting ready to see Tony Bennett sing "Fly Me to the Moon" a cappella at Carnegie Hall.

My biggest fear in writing about New York is that I don't believe it can really be put into words. Even Woody Allen couldn't do it in the opening sequence of his movie *Manhattan*. Walt Whitman tried it with "Crossing Brooklyn Ferry." It's beautiful, let me read it to you.

> *What is it then between us?*
> *I too walk'd the streets of Manhattan island, and bathed*
>   *in the waters around it,*
> *I too felt the curious abrupt questionings stir within me,*
> *In the day among crowds of people sometimes they came*
>   *upon me,*
> *Ah, what can ever be more stately and admirable to me*
>   *than mast-hemm'd Manhattan?*

I can feel what Walt was getting at deep down in my soul, but I don't really know what he was saying!

So here's my attempt:

As far back as I can remember . . . I can remember
Manhattan.

Some of my first memories in life are of being dragged through Chinatown, Little Italy, and Jew Town by my very hyperactive, very Brooklyn-like Manhattan-loving mother. After my always-promised fortune cookies on Mott Street and chocolate-covered jellies on Orchard she'd run me ragged from Canal down to Chambers Street in search of that ultimate bargain down nobody-but-she-knew backstreets, then walk me clear uptown and sometimes even over the 59th Street Bridge and home. My mother loved knowing New York and nobody knew it like her. Oh, and the Chinese apples on Essex.

After complaining for years about all those long walks I did what most kids do when they get old enough to go out on their own. I followed right in her footsteps. Literally. There were times when we even ran into each other on our separate journeys through New York:

"Hey Ma, what are you doing here?"

"What do ya mean me? What are you doing here?"

I've spent more days and nights walking up and down this city than you could imagine. A few of them alone but most with friends. Our nightly journeys consisted of lots of strange short-stay pit stops, some of them regular but most found by chance.

On Monday nights our place was the Speakeasy club on MacDougal Street. Monday was open-mike night and just about every lunatic in this city in dire need of unleashing their insanity in front of an audience would sign their name up, and when called could either play two songs or do eight minutes of anything they wanted on stage. And when you advertise that anybody-can-do-anything-they-want on MacDougal Street you get nothing short of what you ask for.

I have seen everything in there from bad, bad, horrible magic (if we ever meet ask me and I'll show you the trick), to surprisingly good folk songs, to a woman being dragged off stage after finding that her eight minutes—an outlet for her inferno of hatred, violently lashing out at the audience about her "Mother fucking NEVER ENDING URINARY TRACT INFECTION!"—were not enough.

One Monday, among all the bad comedians and transplanted subway musicians, we joined in. At around midnight, one by one we were called. Me, Jimmy, Mike O'Shea, and Danny all went up to try a few new songs out. Ray, our other friend and Monday night Speakeasy comedian, began and ended his eight-minute monologue in thirty seconds with a very droning and dark, "Hi, my name is Ray and my hobbies include inhaling and exhaling . . . thank you."

Just as we were sure that Ray's was probably the best act of the night our other friend, E.J., was called up to the stage. When the announcer asked him if he was doing comedy or needed a guitar he very seriously, calmly, and sure of himself in a low voice asked if he could play a cassette recording through the sound system while he talked. The announcer said OK. E.J. took out a box and stood at the microphone using his stool as a sort of show-and-tell table. Adjusting the microphone, he continued on in his low, serious voice, "Hello my name is E.J. and I am here to invite you to dinner." He took out a plate, knife, and fork, and set it down on the stool. The audience, paying hardly any mind to him, talked among themselves. Knowing E.J. had some sort of strangeness on the way, and having wondered all night what was inside the very secretive brown paper bags he was carrying, we prepared ourselves.

As he went on, teasing about what was for dinner, he began capturing the attention of a few members of the audience. He then placed the two paper bags on the table. As he looked into the bags, he slowly and quietly said, "Oh, and what do we have here?" "Mmm, what do we have here?" All of a sudden the tape blasted this complete high-frequency ear-piercing tone (the kind you hear in an old '70s horror movie when the killer jumps out) and E.J. fell over the table screaming "OH MY GOD!" and threw one bag full of locusts that he had gotten from a pet store all over everyone. From the other bag he took a lamb's head he had just brought from the butcher shop and began hacking at it with a meat cleaver, splattering blood all over himself and the audience.

Everyone in the club ran out except for us. We were laughing so hard that we couldn't even move. E.J. was thrown out and told that bugs and stabbing meat weren't included in the "anything" clause.

Although all of our nights were not as monumental as this one, they were each at the very least unique.

On our journeys uptown along the West Side we'd sometimes climb up the old abandoned train station on Little West 12th Street to drink, and peek in on the always-entertaining S&M members of the Hell Fire Club. And there were always the transvestite prostitutes on West 15th Street strutting their well-choreographed Marilyns and Mansfields to our endless barrage of stink bombs. Our favorite was a heavily bearded and mustached he-she who seemed to make no effort to fool anyone at all beyond the minimal effort of a dollar-fifty blonde Orchard Street wig. We'd then head up to 33rd and Park to watch the straight beautiful lost Southern Janes all waltz down Park Avenue like a sea of sad misguided doves trying hard to hide their rich Midwestern dysfunctional feathers. But if you wanted the real deal, and we often did, the spent Puerto Rican queens on 8th Avenue were never too far away.

Forty-second Street was almost an every night stop. There were the peep shows, preferably Show World on 42nd and 8th, but if darkness was what you were looking for there were always the more offbeat of the offbeat ones along 8th, as well as the upstairs back-room green door theaters. One very memorable experience, at around fifteen years old, was talking our way into a show named "Dr. Bizarro" at Peep Land that included a midget, live fish, free coffee and doughnuts (no joke), and the most beautiful brunette all strung out and gone dancing lost to "California Dreamin'." (Eddie I know you remember.)

Our journeys uptown were not without price though, for the trek through Mike O'Shea's desert was a requirement. Mike O'Shea, one of our nightly wanderers, had appropriately named the area between 14th Street and 42nd "The Desert." Below 14th there was always life—clubs, all-night delis, and lots of people. The same was true above 42nd, but on those long walks through the 7th Avenue Twenties or 6th Avenue Thirties, there was nothing but "The Desert."

At the last deli on 14th Street, before entering The Desert, we would stop for some snacks and joke about hoping we'd make it through. Our midnight journeys would then begin as we moved through the quiet Twenties daytime flower district madness and the barren-as-of-8-P.M. Thirties, while the Macy's crowd, all fast asleep at home, dreamed of their mad street-filled tomorrows. Our only "Oasis" came at 33rd and 7th, the Penta Hotel, now a Ramada Inn. We used to sneak in the back door and head up to the twelfth floor to a guest room that was open all night with couches, a TV with a cable box, and a complimentary coffee machine.

The Penta was one of three "houses" or rest stops that we would spend lots of time in, the other two being the Plaza's second mezzanine, where there was a similar room with a big white piano, and the 37th floor of the new Marriott on 45th and Broadway.

At the Penta's ballroom on the third and fourth floors, we crashed every type of event, from a party for Guy Lombardo, Jr., with the London Philharmonic Orchestra playing, to some esoteric real weird late-night conventions of people "feeling each other," to Jewish bar mitzvahs. It was a haven for the absurd, the unusual, and us. And, usually, free food.

One night at the Penta about fifteen of us got together with some Old English and White Castles to go have a party on the twelfth floor. When we got there a guard (concierge) was sitting inside the guest room. We took the back freight elevators downstairs to the ballroom, which was completely empty, and had our party there. We locked all the doors, plugged a radio into the wall, and had the best time (go there now and you will hear echoes of "Sheena Is a Punk Rocker").

My memories of all those late night adventures are among the very best in my life. The dreaminess of Lincoln Center at night, the quiet of sitting by a nobody's-around fountain on 6th Avenue and 53rd Street, the chance of running into a midnight parade rehearsal in midtown on the eve of a holiday, or just the beauty of the transvestites, hookers, pimps, crazies, wanderers, and all the other irreplaceable artifacts of a city's midnight. New York's midnight. (It's as easy as getting a soda at the McDonald's on 46th and Broadway at 2 A.M. on a Monday night and sitting on the upper level by the giant window, it's clean! Just look out at it all. It's there. I promise.) And where else could you accidentally trip into a Buddhist shrine in Chinatown at two in the morning, be invited to a party by two beautiful girls (one the singer Suzanne Vega's sister) and end up in the middle of a sort of ceremony chanting "Nam-myoho-renge-kyo" barefoot for hours, or call (212) 255-2748 because it was scribbled down a back alley on Ludlow Street and begin a lifelong relationship with an underground group of faceless confessors called Apology. Call it, see for yourself. (Unfortunately, "Mr. Apology" has since died and the line has been disconnected.)

And saints! Are you kidding? This city's nights are full of them. There's Michael on MacDougal Street, a real beat-looking character in his fifties, aimlessly talking absolute unclear nonsense in his unique poetic way. The last time I ran into him, among his berserk rambling I managed to make out a sort of greeting that sounded like, "Hey the last time I saw you, you were hollering Maria out a window with a shotgun in one hand and two record covers in the other." There's an unnamed deepest baritone saint who resides in front of Trash and Vaudeville on Saint Mark's Place with the kindest smile in the world, occupying most of his time flipping coffee container lids high up in the air like boomerangs and catching them while telling you that it's "Time to Pray!" There's Irving on the West Side eager to tell you about his part in New York's 1950s while the soprano belts out his best Pavarotti on West 57th Street between 6th and 7th.

There are heroes and poets and musicians and madmen and they're all out there waiting for you. But take my advice, you won't find them on the main roads. Well, maybe you will. Definitely you will. But it will have to be late. It will have to be dark. Like looking for deer. It will have to be when no one's around. You'll have to blend in. You will have to be one of them. One of us.

And if you wanna find it, this is what you do. It's what my mother would tell you to do. "You go out. You get a dollar, a dollar twenty-five or whatever a subway ride may cost you now. You get a token and go downtown. All the way down. You go out now. And get lost. Get real lost. But have fun with it. You never do know who or what you may run into."

And the vision was quick. As quick as it was vivid. And it was of you. Of you and me walking down a jazz-filled Miles Davis Saint Mark's Place. "So What" (especially once the trumpet kicks in). And just as that vision faded, the sweetest sound of a pleading Curtis Mayfield took us all the way up to 111th Street (Eddie you should know better). Oh, and that was where we kissed . . . Annette. Where we kissed that magic kiss and wrote poems where every line rhymed. And being this was all a vision, a dream, a daydream, well then we went back downtown with The Isley Brothers "Who's That Lady" filling up all the empty cracks along 8th Avenue's 1970s spent red-lit bars (around 38th Street). And Tony Bennett owned Mulberry Street as an Art Pepper saxophone gently put our hearts to rest on a snowy Central Park Christmas. We got high, crazy crazy high on Leonard Street to "Suzanne" but that got scary so I wished Lou Reed's "Coney Island Baby" to take us back up Elizabeth, especially that part where he says, "Man, you know I'd give it all up for you." And then the Tibetan bells clanged, and the vision ended. And Danny Styles's AM 1050 seven nights a week forever talk show was right there in Eddie's car . . . a Camaro . . . a Camaro with a red light in it and a thick brown rug . . . And all those daydreams and visions were now slowly being consumed by Danny Styles's endless and I mean endless talk of kielbasa, knishes, pork chops, pierogies, and just food in general (the man speaks all night, seven a week of nothing but food).

Well just as I could bear no more I switched on CBS's Cousin Bruuuuceeey, to the sound of Dion's "The Wanderer."

Eddie, it's time to go home.

photo: Xavier Cruz

guide to recognizing your saints

Memorable quote from Jimmy about this photograph of E.J. driving in Central Park with a family in the back: "If they only knew they just paid $38 to a driver who would (even if he had to sacrifice himself) gladly drive them into eternal darkness forever."

Mike O'Shea at Penta "House" crashed party under strange circumstances.

MAYBERRY, INDIANA, ON HIGHWAY 1

we were driving on Highway 1 from San Francisco to Los Angeles (the long way) in a big giant red pickup truck. It was me, Ray, Matty O'Brian, and four other friends of ours from New York.

About three hours south of San Francisco we ran across this really wild traveling carnival in the middle of nowhere. We spent the whole night there on broken-down unsafe 1950s-looking Ferris wheels, and playing impossible softball in toilet-seat games, trying so hard to win that giant stuffed teddy bear with a Budweiser shirt on that we knew would win the heart of the prettiest green-eyed Mexican girl you ever did see for the night, but always ending up with that same old horrible dehydrated stuffed snake consolation prize.

After about three hours, five candy apples, four bags of cotton candy, and not much luck, we decided to head on. As we were pulling away, almost perfectly diagonal to us was this wild Tiffany's moon out just laying quietly across this real yellow, almost mustard-looking sky. From the back of our pickup truck we could see the carnival lights all going out one by one, very slowly, as if only one guy was walking to each section shutting them off. There was that real dreamy kind of sad surreal feeling that you always seem to get at the end of a long day at an amusement park, and the fact that we were all together, a little drunk, and heading nowhere made it all that much more dramatic.

In the front seat Matty, Laurie, Joanne McGerty, and Mikey Dallas were all bunched up together laughing and trying to stop Johnny from taking a leak out of the passenger side window. Me and my friend Ray, whom I have known since kindergarten at P.S. 85 in Queens, were the only two sitting out in the back. Not usually much of a poet, though Highway 1, a few shots of cheap carnival vodka, and the back of a pickup truck could probably turn anyone into one, he described perfectly the mountains on both sides of us looking like a thousand sleeping Doberman pinschers lying all over each other. Then, even more unlike Ray, with the poetic enthusiasm of ten thousand eternal youths, he yelled, "Ain't this great!" and I knew just what he meant. It wasn't just the mountains, or being drunk, or the laughing coming from the front. It was everything. It was freedom. Being free. Just out there, nowhere, nothing, youth.

69

FOURTEEN DAYS
WITH A CRAZY
INDIAN
MODERN-DAY
SAINT

i drove fourteen days and two thousand miles through the Joshua trees of two California deserts. I was in love with a crazy Indian modern-day saint, Lisa Marie.

We started out on Hollywood and Vine in a beat-up old '70s Chevrolet homemade convertible (roof was sawed off) that my friend John Wiley was about to junk. I had saved up about four hundred dollars unloading trucks on the 11th Avenue Jacob Javitz docks in Manhattan. Along with the money I had saved from an "I Love New York" commercial in which I can be seen dancing to the "Electric Boogie," disastrously drunk next to Governor Mario Cuomo, and a spread Lisa had just done for *Playboy,* we were pretty set for a while.

In Los Angeles she told me about a place that was only three hours away called "Joshua Tree." She said it was beautiful, mysterious, romantic, and that it was right smack in the middle of the Mojave Desert.

We left on a Friday night. After driving for about two and a half hours we pulled over at a little all-night truck stop. It was three in the morning and out of pure excitement neither of us were even remotely tired yet. We parked right at the foot of two gigantic cement dinosaurs that were out there to attract passersby. We got out of our car to the sound of faraway laughter and the low rumbling of about fourteen engine-running parked eighteen-wheelers. It was a late-night truck stop symphony, surrounded by absolute silence. As we walked toward the diner the sensation of absolute and complete free-dom hit me like a thousand pillows. It was freedom at a 3 A.M. nowhere. After two hamburgers and about three plates of deli-ciously way-overcooked french fries we got back out on the road again.

When we finally arrived at our destination it was pitch-black out. We pulled into a small twenty-two-dollar motel called the Joshua Tree Motel, and had our choice of any room we wanted. Room four, my lucky number. I stayed up for nearly an hour watching a static-ridden evangelist coming through a broken old black-and-white TV, aside tired Lisa lying beautiful asleep among the beat and raggedy off-orange bedspread.

When morning came I walked outside to see where we were. It was an unbelievable sight. The sky was forever, bluer and bigger than any sky I had ever seen. I got so excited I ran inside, woke Lisa, and we headed straight out to nowhere with our convertible wide open and down.

After driving through what I can only describe as a kind of Flintstones meets Mars, we saw a sign that said:

LAS VEGAS>>>

Without stopping to think we followed the arrows onto Highway 15 and took it all the way to Nevada.

Half a day later Las Vegas was cool but it wasn't what we were looking for. We stopped for two quick $1.99 dinners at a casino called The Golden Nugget and headed on, out of the lights.

We got lost for a while before ending up on the old famous Route 66 and decided to go in the direction of Arizona. We drove all night on 66 drinking Store 24 Strawberry Riunite with nothing but the sounds of occasional freight trains, coyotes, and believe it or not a Frankie Valli special on the only radio station we could pick up.

We found a youth hostel in a town called Tuba City, Arizona. It was a sort-of-hotel for travelers and lost wanderers that charged three dollars and a chore for a night's sleep. Next morning, after vacuuming and pouring tea for about twenty fellow roamers, we were on our way again.

At around two-thirty in the morning, what sounded like a beautiful wind in the key of an Ennio Morricone D 7th woke me up. I followed the sound to one big shower that all the men at the hostel shared. When I went inside, there were about fifteen Native Americans hanging around, showering and playing this real dreamy-sounding wooden wind instrument called a pan flute. One of the men who had seen me with my guitar the night before asked if I would go get it and sing religious songs with them. We spent the whole morning singing at least twenty different versions of "Amazing Grace" together naked. Lisa eventually woke up and came knocking on the bathroom door wondering what the hell was going on. When I opened it, naked, mid-chorus with our whole congregation, she almost died hysterical laughing. We all went to eat breakfast together outside at a long picnic table. A member of the Navajo nations named Jim Coyote gave my girl a rope necklace, told me that she was sunshine, happiness, and that I . . . well, needed to learn more songs. I talked about New York and my own Mike O'Shea 14th Street desert that no one understood while everyone there told us about what seemed like a different planet.

After our long great interesting breakfast we said good-bye to our new friends and headed onward toward New Mexico on an alternative route that a friend of ours in New York, Jonathan Elias, had told us would bring us right through the Hopi and Navajo reservations.

Our route took us through a town in Arizona called Santa Claus, population: 10. It consisted of one buffalo, ten people, and five houses in the middle of the desert—all lit up and decorated for Christmas. The population sign read:

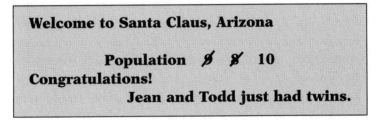

Welcome to Santa Claus, Arizona

Population 10
Congratulations!
Jean and Todd just had twins.

We stopped for a quick picture with the buffalo and headed on through a string of other towns. A few miles past Bedrock City (which looked like the Flintstones lived there) we stopped at Nick's, a little pizza shop off the side of the road. Nick, the owner, was from Greece so when I told him that I was from Astoria, Queens (third-largest Greek population on earth) he almost had a heart attack. It turned out that he had lived only about three blocks away from me for about two years. Neither of us could believe it. He brought his whole family out of a trailer in the back to join us for some pizza and wine. I asked him what had made him go to such a remote place. "The business," he laughed, pointing out to the endless empty dirt road. He then looked more serious and said "Love, peace, and family." Lisa and I told Nick he was either a "good" or "very wanted" man. We shook hands, and I promised that I would tell everybody back in Astoria about the best pizza in the desert.

We headed to New Mexico. Lisa put a tape of the *Billy the Kid* soundtrack in a junky old boom box our friend John had given us since the car's tape player was broken. The sky was wide open and it was a great day.

We were slowed down by everything from cows crossing the roads to a bunch of wild horses running free. We ate at Navajo Joe's Tacos and Harry's Desert Dogs, drank from natural running mineral springs, and stopped at one Hopi reservation.

Two little kids named Glendora and Larry tried to sell me a bow without an arrow for five dollars. I told them I'd take it if it came with a tour. They took us around and showed us where the chief lived and the homes of their medicine man and local elders. They showed us the area where their ceremonies took place, but said they weren't old enough to take part in them yet. I traded Larry my NY Mets baseball cap for a walk through the underground churches that his people had made to protect them in case of hurricanes. The clay walls of the tunnels were all lavender and orange. Candles lit up beautiful detailed hand-made crucifixes and other religious articles. At the far end we saw real ceremonial American-eagle feathered costumes. I felt like Tom Sawyer or a surfaced Jacques Cousteau. When we came out of the tunnel we saw, on top of an adobe castle, about an arm's-length away, eight perched American eagles. I couldn't believe it. I pulled out this real cheesy disposable camera I got back in Las Vegas to get a picture, but Glendora told me the chief didn't allow pictures to be taken on the reservation. "He says, 'the greatest pictures will live forever in your memory.'" Glendora and the chief were right. We took Larry and Glendora's address, promised to write, and returned to the road.

NEW MEXICO >>>

An hour later, under our beautiful clean sky, out of nowhere came the most terrifying black lightning-filled cloud I had ever seen. It rolled in right over us as if we were driving right into the hellish mouth of a volcano. The thunder was so loud and strong that it shook the entire car. Lightning was striking everywhere. There were no cars, stores, or anything for as far as we could see.

For one split second I got out of the car to try and have Lisa take a once-in-a-lifetime picture of me standing on the roof of it with lightning striking all around me. And in that split second I came to the realization that like it or not I was a New Yorker, and death by mugger beats death by Mother Nature in the desert . . . any day. So we jumped back inside and drove on.

Just as quick as we rode into the storm we drove out of it. From the rearview mirror we could still see the giant dark clouds roaring on. A reminder that this was still God's land.

As a new, more peaceful darkness came over us we decided to head on toward a town called Ojo Caliente ("the hot eye"). On our way there, a truck drove past us with a license plate that read, "New Mexico, Land of Enchantment." It was the first time I had ever seen the state license plate and it seemed a strange motto.

There were two routes to Ojo Caliente. One was a safe two-hour route down newly paved roads. The other would only take forty-five minutes, but was made for four-wheel-drive pickup trucks. We took the short way only to find after twenty minutes of driving that the road had become so steep we couldn't go more than one mile an hour without sliding off the edge. Turning around was impossible as the road we were crawling on, which wound slowly down and around an enormous mountain, was barely wide enough for all four wheels of the car to fit on at the same time. After three hours of our shortcut we found a small shoulder and decided to pull over and sleep.

When the sunlight shining off a "Danger Falling Rocks" sign woke me up the next morning I couldn't believe what we had been driving on in pitch darkness. The road above and below us was even narrower than I had thought. But what a sight. We were on the very edge of an enormous rock mountain. About a mile down you could see a thin water stream. It was one of the most incredible places I had ever seen. The sounds and colors of the strangest and most beautiful noisy butterflies I had ever seen were everywhere, along with the scent of sandalwood.

One night, five hours, and the coolest post office in the middle of nowhere later, Ojo Caliente was well worth the trip. It was a tiny little very friendly Native American village. We sat outside by the food shop and ate beans and rice. After about twenty minutes of Game Boy with my new friend, Johnny Elk, he told me about a hot spring that he worked at just down the road. It was a big ditch in the ground filled with natural hot water that people come to relax and meditate in. If I was interested he would show it to me.

When we got there the first step was to shower in this big lunchroom-looking place. Then, completely naked, we joined about five other people in the hot spring. One giant overweight-looking cowboy from across the water yelled over, laughing and loud, "Drink the water! It's good for you, got iron in it!" and dunked his head under this unbelievably hot water. He told me that once a year he takes a week off work, places "a piss bucket between the gas and the brake," drives here nonstop from San Francisco, and then forgets about everything. Everyone else there had similar stories of escaping and searching.

After about twenty-five minutes of drinking and boiling in the hot iron water spring, for fear of death I had to get out. The cowboy, on the other hand, somehow completely unaffected by the scorching steaming hot water, had managed to fall fast asleep. Johnny Elk, laughing, told me that our cowboy friend was "malo en la cabeza" (crazy in the head). Johnny told me to lie down on a long, firm mattress, where I was wrapped from head to toe in wool. Every five minutes he would come, lift the wool from my face to wipe my sweat and feed me some iron water. After twenty minutes under the wool and one freezing-cold shower the ritual was over.

We went outside and sat on two big orange-painted stones. I asked Johnny how much I owed him, and he asked me how I felt. "Great!" I said. He said "five bucks," and went on to tell me the meaning of the ritual. "Some people use it as a way of getting closer and becoming more aware of God." I asked if that was why he went. "Oh, I like what it does to my skin. I go to a church to pray!" I laughed. Imitating my voice he asked, "So, is the Empire State Building all it's cracked up to be or what?" We laughed as I then went on, as always, telling him about my home. While we were talking, a bald eagle flew by us and perched on top of a fenced roof. I freaked and told Johnny Elk that before this trip the freest bird I'd ever seen was a pigeon. Not surprised at all by the eagle he told me that the fenced roof was its home. It was always flying back and forth there. I told him I still thought it was pretty incredible. He asked if I still went wild every time I passed the Empire State Building. I kind of understood what he meant.

When it was time to move on, I promised Johnny Elk I would never walk by the Empire State Building again without looking up, if he promised to do the same with the eagle. We shook hands on it and said good-bye.

On our journey, which would soon bring us to a town called Taos, I began thinking a lot about the people and sights and experiences we had come across in the last few days. I felt like I was beginning to understand a lot of things that I had never understood before. I had always heard about the unfair treatment of the Native Americans, but as I went from town to town, meeting and talking and eating with the people there, my eyes began to open. I began noticing expiration dates on the milk and lots of other foods in their supermarkets were way past due. Their vegetables and fruits were so dehydrated that you couldn't even give them away in any of our major cities. I remembered when I was a kid how much I hated when the free cheese we used to get from the government was green with mold. At least half of their houses didn't even have roofs on them, and while our senators and local, often crooked, politicians are vacationing at their summer homes in the Bahamas after determining whether or not the minimum wage should be raised, the people here are having ceremonies, paying tribute, and thanking God for his kindness and generosity from their humble, half-broken-down clay huts, the best ones on the reservations.

Oppression was a word I played with back and forth in my mind. It's obvious the people here suffer from it, but the fact that any people, not just Native American people, can be treated so unfairly in a country with so much to offer makes it all that much worse. I know how easy it is to sound like a corny version of Noam Chomsky when talking about something like this, but in a country where millions of dollars are spent on nuclear weapons, corporate welfare, and many ridiculous things, doesn't it just make sense to take care of people first? As soon as we can make the South Bronx, Compton, Taos, and Astoria look like Beverly Hills I'll have no problem watching a guy orbit Mars.

These places I've mentioned are contaminated with oppression, and you've got to know that it affects you in every way. It is a disease that enters your lifestyle, mind, and spirit, spreads, and eventually kills. Its cause is neglect, selfishness, ignorance, and prejudice. Its only cure will be love, understanding, caring, and action. You know what? . . . Just be a liberal. A real, true, bleeding-heart liberal. There you go, just do it, you'll be so glad you did.

Half a day later we pulled into Taos, New Mexico around midnight on a Thursday. After unsuccessfully looking for a youth hostel for about an hour, tired, we pulled up to a wild-looking motel called The Laughing Horse Inn. What looked like an apparition wearing a long thin white cotton robe let us in.

His name was Santos. He was a real frail, light-skinned, Spanish-looking black man about five-foot-four with the kindest face you've ever seen. With his real faint, whispery voice he asked us where we were from and offered us some tea.

The Laughing Horse was a hippie-built kind of bed and breakfast house with about eight different rooms where guests could stay. Right in the center was one big living room with one of the most incredible video, record, and book collections I had ever seen. There was everything from Jack Kerouac's *On the Road* to the Sex Pistols' *Never Mind the Bollocks* to a movie called *Let's Get Lost* that our New York friend, Bruce Weber, had made starring Chet Baker and my girl, Lisa Marie.

The sounds of a quiet, cool Miles Davis softly whispering out of strangely placed homemade speakers could be heard all throughout The Laughing Horse, accompanied by the dreamy, sweet scent of light smoking sage incense.

The rooms were each unexplainably decorated. Georgia O'Keeffe, as well as a bunch of other painters and writers, had lived here in the past, and you could definitely feel that. The aura was somewhere between a hipster's community log cabin and a biblical scene straight out of "The Twilight Zone." We finally settled on a small cozy room with a purple light in it. There was a giant, thick, wooden Paul Bunyan–looking ladder leading up to the top half of our bunk beds with one small circular window really unusually placed. I dreamed that Santos told us that the entire moon would fit right into it if you lay correctly on the bed, on a full-moon night.

The price for staying at The Laughing Horse was twenty dollars a night plus fifty cents for ice creams, beers, or sodas. TV dinners were $1.25. You were trusted entirely to check off the amounts you had eaten on a chalkboard with all the guests' names.

We spent most of the night exploring The Laughing Horse until we stumbled into a hidden trap-door sauna in the back of our room. It had a radio speaker in it, and when we turned a freaky old switch to "on," both the radio and heat began flooding the room. At around 100 degrees we made crazy love to the Rolling Stones' "Beast of Burden."

When morning came we were awakened by the sweetest scent of banana cake accompanied by low breakfast talk and laughter from the other guests in the living room. We went out and joined them for a delicious breakfast compliments of Santos in honor of his new guests, us. It was real weird. The people were so friendly. A few of them lived there for parts of the year while the others seemed to be regular long-staying guests. They acted like one big family and were very interested in meeting us and showing us around Taos. It could have almost gotten spooky, like *The Stepford Wives*, but it didn't. We had the best time and ended up staying for almost a week.

After wandering aimlessly through four states and two deserts in less than two weeks it was really fun to come home each night, play Monopoly in the perfect living room with a big new friendly adopted family, and then cuddle up in our top bunk and watch *Harold and Maude* on a freaked-out mini-television. The people staying there were all very interesting. A lot of them were wanderers just like us. Looking. Searching for something. A place where you could just smile and laugh and joke and eat cake and hot chocolate.

The Laughing Horse Inn, at the end of our great great enlightening journey was that place, and forever, whenever I can, or you can find the time to, we should go. But please, please take the long way there.

Meanwhile back home . . .
Completely gone   lost
can't even find good right words
Eddie's car   Camaro   '75 Beat Brown
red light inside   dark   moody   tin foil everywhere
even scary a little

nothing on radio but dark dark darkest scary maybe
     even cool blues
               all down   down beat   way down

keep that dial below 90 it's those 89 fm's that get you
     here
just watching deserted Queens 47th road
no sign of my Saints anywhere
man crazy crazy moody darkest blue ever
     and it's right now
     this second
yes now   here   passing 43rd onward ⟶

and no one is talking
cause everyone is flying
and the scary music is blasting blaring screaming crying
     pleading
all under this reddest light
and it's right now
and I love it and I hate it and I'm scared of it and I
          wanna be able to comeback here
and I don't know if I'll ever get this far here again

82

This ain't no Mayberry
Desperation   Desolation   Nothing Broke
too broke for even the subway
hungry   not even drunk
thinking about going to The Door   maybe even the
    Under 21
Damn, even Father Ritter is in trouble!
miss her who's far away and no longer loves me
miss him   miss my friends
bad coke deals are going down at the Blarney Stone on 8th
    Jimmy near death   Lisa so sad

Don't even wanna hear Tom Waits
    bluer than Chet Baker
boring old sad jazz just makes sense now
        loss for words
can't even imagine a rhyme
and man if it wasn't so damn hot
DOWN AND OUT   REALLY REALLY
lost
not a good day
    sad blue day
maybe Eddie will come with that $5.
    we'll just go roam around Downtown
that would make it better

you will take no more life from me
you will not slow down my natural instincts
you will not make my loud hysterical hissing laugh
    muffled
you will always keep me younger than all my baseball
    heroes, too young to order coffee at chock
    full o' nuts, too young to open a newspaper in a
    crowded subway
you will rationalize no more dreams
you will take no more dear friends from me

you will not disappear any more vivid memories or fade
away melancholy technical insignificant but perfect
moments
the way her bottom lip quivered in my hallway rain
pouring outside lamppost light only light
you will put no more distance between us
you will not hurt me any more
for from this day on i will begin learning to live
with you
i will allow you to give so much more to me
and i wish this was all true
but it isn't
well maybe a little
but you will just keep doing all of these things to me

won't you

**freaks,
bizarres,
friends, living
obscenities**

guide to recognizing your saint

ANGELO
RUGGIERA

everybody was there, the whole neighborhood was dressed up. I was back in Astoria, small talk was happening, and then Nerf turned to me and said, "Look at Angelo just lying there, he looks like he still had something left to do."

Nerf then reminded me of the time Angelo made it to the top of the Grease Pole at the Saint Rocco feast. The Grease Pole was a telephone pole that they would put in the middle of the feasts at the Bohemian Hall and cover with grease. All the men would take their shirts off and try to climb it. If you got to the top you got one hundred dollars. At different levels were cheeses, prosciutto, and wine bottles.

While Angelo mesmerized everyone by climbing to the top, we robbed all the stuffed-animal prizes and mirrors with rock band names from behind the Italian band doing a cover of Laura Branigan's "Gloria." I remembered it as well as Nerf did. Those were good times.

Then I heard someone else say, "Hey, it sucks, but you live that way, you die that way," as someone else in disbelief muttered, "How could Graziano pull that trigger after all the years we've all known each other?"

And all I kept thinking about was Heaven, and me and Antonio many years ago laughing at his little brother Angelo, running up and down the stoop naked and crying away from his mother, and how nice it would be for all of us to see each other like this every once in a while without a funeral taking place.

And the message was not to let go, but to move on.

GUTTERBOY

andy warhol had just died. There was going
to be this big remembrance celebration in his honor downtown
at an outdoor street festival on Rivington Street. Deborah Harry,
Ultra Violet, Taylor Mead, Jean-Michel Basquiat, The Talking
Heads, Lou Reed, and just about every hip famous New Yorker
at the time was supposed to be there. Somehow my band,
Gutterboy, had gotten on the bill to play. It was going to be our
first show ever. It was on a Saturday and we were to be the first
band going on at about three in the afternoon.

The day of the show I met our bass player, John Wiley, a
skinny, pigeon-toed, hot-pink-haired fellow crazy in front of his

job at Trash and Vaudeville on St. Mark's Place. We were standing outside from about 10 A.M. until noon waiting for our drummer, Chuck, to show up.

Around noon something started smelling real bad. It was a stench that could have knocked you out. We didn't know what it was. All of a sudden a bunch of police cars pulled up and started sifting through the garbage cans right across the street from us in front of a place called "Enz." What, or maybe who, I should say, they found was the girlfriend of a guy named Daniel Rakowitz. Daniel Rakowitz was a local St. Mark's dealer freak who worked as a short-order cook on Perry Street. One day I guess he decided to chop up his girlfriend, cook her, and put the rest of her in "Enz" garbage cans right across from me and John on the night before our first show. These things happen. A quote in the *Daily News* after his arrest read, "I killed her and boiled her head."

Our drummer never showed up, but we walked on over to Rivington Street anyway. On the way over we ran into a friend of ours named Joey Dancing. Joey Dancing was about six-foot-three, always smiling, and a great drummer whom I used to play with in a hardcore band called Major Conflict.

The reason me and Joey Dancing weren't playing together anymore was because for the last seven years, due to heavy amounts of angel dust, quaaludes, alcohol, and crack cocaine, he had become convinced that he was the musician Prince. For a short while he stopped being Prince, and was the son of Prince and Marilyn Monroe. (In moments of half-clarity, whenever the thorazine would wear off, he would explain, "If you're gonna have a nervous breakdown you might as well be Marilyn Monroe's kid.") At one time or another, Joey Dancing had thought that Prince was out to kill him, that Joey Dancing had to kill Prince, and that I, an Irish-Nicaraguan white kid from Queens, had become Prince myself. After several mental institutions and about five years of thorazine we decided that maybe it was a good time for us to start looking in different directions (bigger bands call this "irreconcilable differences"). Well on this day, years later, the day of our big show, we needed a drummer and since Joey Dancing was there we decided to give it a try.

Me, John Wiley, and Joey Dancing got to Rivington Street at about three in the afternoon. No one was there. Well, when I say "no one" I am exaggerating a bit. There of course were the street drunks, you know, the ones who show up to every out-door festival and never stop dancing to the sounds of anything, preferably salsa or mambo, with their bottles of Night Train and Thunderbird. There were the local Ludlow Street transvestites sitting out on stoops working on their three-in-the-afternoon purple Kool-Aid eye shadow while attempting to ignore the harassment from the little Puerto Rican Indians running through the open fire hydrants where Rivington meets Essex Street. There were the fifteen-member Spanish families on fourth-story fire escapes livening things up with the cool sounds of the romantic José José; and right up front were our only two fans at the time, a pair of identical leathered-out Filipino twins that John Wiley and me were dating at the time. Deborah Harry, Lou Reed, The Talking Heads, or any of them for that matter were nowhere to be found. We went on anyway. Halfway through our first song, "A Rainy Day on Mulberry Street," just as all our drunken Night Train friends were working their slurred salsa dances into our set, Joey Dancing fainted due to an overdose of methadone while I fell off the back of the stage and John Wiley laughed so hard he couldn't continue on the bass.

That was the end of our show, to the dismay of no one. The transvestites, hard at work on their mirrors, never budged, the salsa resumed, the crazies danced, the celebration continued.

Oh . . . and Gutterboy was born.

FREAK MAGNET

john wiley calls me a freak magnet
because of all the strange people who always seem to come in and out of my life and Bob Semen was without a doubt at the top of that list. The timing of his arrival was perfect. Bob Semen was a sort of Broadway Danny Rose turned crooked Caligula. He was about forty years old, stood five-foot-eight with flaming red hair and a giant red barbershop-quartet Rip Taylor mustache. You could usually find him in his signature green and brown high-water suits, over-the-top '70s horrifying hell-bent off-orange mustard turtleneck sweater, somewhere

near an arcade, bus terminal, or other popular runaway haven in midtown.

Bob ran "Star Productions," an unbelievably illegitimate, straight-out false, television movie and modeling business on 52nd Street and Broadway, right upstairs from the Kit Kat Club.

His clients included every type of person—midgets pumping money into him for new head shots that endlessly printed out of focus (fifty dollars a roll) in hope of being cast as the new Tattoo in the "reunion" of *Fantasy Island* that "only" Bob knew about (he being so connected), and old women opening up their checkbooks in hopes of being the next "Where's the beef?" lady.

I met Bob Semen on the corner of 45th and Broadway while working at a stand for Larry's Fresh Fruit Ices, when he bought a piña colada–flavored large ice ("and don't give me the mushy part!"). He told me I'd make more money if I took the corner where they sell theater tickets. Soon after, Bob took over as manager of Gutterboy. In those three months we were promised everything from the cover of *Rolling Stone* to the lead in his new ten-million-dollar movie, *No More Mistakes*, about the man who invented the pencil eraser. "You know, in the vein of that Harrison Ford *Tucker* crap!"

95

Bob Semen's big budget for *No More Mistakes* never came in. The cover of *Rolling Stone*, our feature in *Time,* and all our other major press articles were also on hold indefinitely. He did manage to get our picture in the window of the video arcade on 53rd Street and Broadway, as well as arrange three separate write-ups in a "singles only" paper geared mainly toward pimps, hookers, johns and he-she's. The schemes that Bob would come up with were incredible. We tried everything from an attempt at breaking into a live "David Letterman" show, which Bob was sure would get us tons of great publicity, to being arrested on the 17th floor of the CBS building after sneaking up to the president of the record label's office with acoustic guitars and accidentally ending up on the "live" news filming floor where Bob threatened an anchor man: let us on "live" or suffer the consequences someday when "we are in demand!" One time I asked him why we didn't just record some songs for a demo and send them around like everyone else. In his always selective choice of words he explained, "Because you stink! I mean all that music stinks, who the hell do you think you are? The Beatles? We gotta do something crazy here!" He'd then go on with his never-ending story about how Elvis stunk too but Colonel Tom Parker, Elvis's manager ("Now, that guy was a genius!") would pay off girls to faint so that he'd look good.

There was something exciting and dark and scary roaming around with Bob and his entourage of freaks through all his crazy peep-show runs and 3 A.M. errands through half-lit whorehouses and his endless "connections in the entertainment field." With Bob we could truly dream over two frankfurters and a papaya for $1.15 on 42nd Street about spending all that money, with all those cars, and all those girls.

Bob Semen is a freak but New York needs freaks. At his best he was hope for the hopeless and at his worst, no more than a lesson. An adventure to be lived and learned.

I went to see Bob about a month ago and was surprised to see that he still had the same office, though the name had changed to "Star Encouragement Entertainment," no doubt after endless *Consumer Affairs* inquires into his half-dozen other names. At first he tried to hit me up with some pitch about some movie I'd be perfect for—something to do with an alien who couldn't talk and gets a job doing some sort of telephone work—"A comedy with a twist!" I stopped Bob in his tracks and reminded him that I was broke. We both laughed and talked for another twenty minutes.

When I went to leave, in a moment of almost true sincerity Bob said, "You know Dito, I really did believe in you, I mean I never took you for any money." I said it was probably because

I didn't have any, but when I looked again, for a moment he almost did seem for real. Just to the left of his always big red smile, hanging all crooked, one thumbtack shy of being just right, I could see "Star Encouragement Entertainment" covering up "Star Productions." I looked at him again and smiled. "Take care of yourself, Bob."

photo: Bob Semen

Bob Semen's office. Upstairs from Kit Kat Club on 52nd Street with Jimmy & Wiley.

a guide to recognizing your saint

BOB SEMEN, FRANK THE DOG WALKER, AND AN OPEN LETTER TO WALT WHITMAN

in california, a beautiful blue-eyed brown-haired girl named Tara just gave me *Leaves of Grass* by Walt Whitman. Before today I only knew him as the guy who has more truck stops in nowhere places named after him than anyone else. Tara told me Whitman was the greatest. I think his poems are pretty good and that Old English tone is starting to grow on me. What I got really hooked on, though, was the foreword. You know, the part where they talk about the writer. Did you know that he used to give himself fake write-ups, print them under alias names, and quote papers that didn't exist to try and sell his book? When he got busted on it once, his explanation was simple and true. "I meant every bit of praise about my book," he said, "but if I used my real name everyone would say that I felt that way only because it was my book." This inspired a letter to Walt.

Dear Mr. Whitman,

Because I just met you today I will temporarily restrain myself from calling you Walt. What you were was a hustler, and wherever you are I would like you to know that immediately upon hearing that story of yours, you have picked up one more fan here on Earth, as I will now return to your book with an entirely different attitude towards you. And if I may have one more moment or a few more paragraphs of your time, let me please elaborate further as to why this story struck such a chord with me. You see, before finding out much about you I had been bored by the name of your book, *Leaves of Grass*, bored by your beard that made you look like a rejected currency model, and bored by your name, Walt. I thought you were an old English major talking in multiple syllables about fairies and evergreens and using *ye's* much too freely. I even spotted a *ye* the first time I scanned your book. But after hearing that story, especially your explanation when you got busted, I realized that not only did I like you, but that I may have even met you in your present reincarnated state. Man, I may have even met many you's . . . *ye's*.

Your present incarnation could quite possibly be my old manager, Bob Semen. You share some quite similar methods, though Bob's are much more 1980s–42nd Street. Let me explain. There used to be a late-night talk show on called "Thicke of the Night." The show was crap, but so absolutely nonentertaining that it actually became entertaining in a disbelieving, trancey sort of way. (You know how that just

99

happens sometimes.) Well as I previously explained (to you, reader) Bob Semen's opinion of our band was pretty straightforward: "You guys stink." But he thought everything stunk, and he was sure that with the right gimmick he could make us superstars. Bob's opinion of entertainers went hand in hand with his belief in reincarnation. As he would put it, "Entertainment people in past lives were either Nazis or extremely well-behaved bugs." So among all of his unbelievable scams for our stardom, the one that stands out far above the rest, the one that even you, Mr. Whitman, I don't believe could have come up with, was the following.

It was a Tuesday. Bob had a big plan. So big he actually took our whole band out for $4.29 steaks (with potatoes) at Tad's on 42nd and paid for them. This was big! Over dinner (we split two orders: "Eat the bread, it'll fill you up") he told us the plan.

With two Betamaxes—the "editing room" in his office on 52nd Street—Bob had concocted a way he was convinced would make people believe we had been the guest band on an episode of the show "Thicke of the Night." I was shocked. I asked what we would do if we gave the forged tape to someone who had actually seen that episode of the show without us on it, and could tell it was a hoax. His always delicate choice of words for an answer was, "First of all, no one ever watches that shit anyway, and even if they did, the fucking show will be off the air so damn fast that they'll have forgotten they ever saw it. He ain't got the durability of Franklin!" (referring to the great Joe Franklin, a WOR TV Channel 9 phenomenon that I won't even attempt to get into).

Bob lined up his two Betamaxes, one loaded with a previously recorded episode of "Thicke of the Night" starring special guest musical sensation Gloria Gaynor, the other loaded with a blank $1.49 tape from Crazy Eddie's on Canal Street. He then strategically cut host Alan Thicke's introduction of Gloria Gaynor and replaced her name with ours, Gutterboy.

Though Bob tried as hard as I'd ever seen him try anything to overdub a good impersonation of Alan Thicke's voice at that key moment, he eventually gave up. The fact that he already had the host mouthing the "G" for Gutterboy in Gloria Gaynor's name kept him frustrated for hours. (I chalk that "G" up as an obvious dig from the Gods.) Exhausted, but never defeated, he devised an alternative that may have been more perfect.

At the moment of Alan Thicke's introduction of Gloria Gaynor, the new editor, Bob Semen, "cut" to a homemade replica of the card that you would normally read leading into a commercial break, but with his slight addition.

It read:

Thicke of the Night Will Be Right Back

The idea was that the viewer would think a commercial had begun too soon, cutting off Alan Thicke's introduction.

Dramatization:

1. Scene 1

Thicke of the night

host
Allen Thicke
↓ " now ladies + gentleman
② = let me please introduce
~~Gutter Boy~~

↳ cut to

2. Scene 2

Static
on your
T.V.

Scene 3

3. BoBs homemade sign
videotaped with his
crappy camera
↓
★ Thicke of the night
will Be right back

with
★ ~~Gutter~~Boy ★

4. Commercials

C&C   Shasta
honk honk McRib

Ajax Crazy eddies
"no talking orangutangs"
"wheres the beef"

5. more
Static
Z
Z
Z

6. Bobsainserted video
badly
↓
thicke of the night
with Gutterboy

After the unexpected commercial "interruptions" Bob spliced
in his own, all-new segment of "Thicke of the Night" which fea-
tured a terribly bad video he had shot of us at our rehearsal studio—which in his opinion looked exactly like Alan Thicke's stage.

Let me say honestly that Bob's collage was so pathetically
bad that even he laughed at it after days of diligent work and

said, with somehow still a far-off notion of a question in his voice, "This is hell, ha?" before forgetting the whole thing.

Later that day, in a compensating manner, Bob used White-Out on a *Rolling Stone* article about a new up-and-coming band, actually handwriting our name in, trying to simulate the magazine's lettering, which his Royale manual typewriter's print was too big for.

Letter to Walt continued

So, Mr. Whitman, all this somehow brings me back to you. As I sit here, now, comparing these somewhat similar yet more technologically advanced hustling methods, I truly wonder if we may have indeed met. If Bob Semen is not your karmic heir, I have another strong candidate.

Tell me Mr. Whitman, does the name Frank Valias ring a bell? How about "Frank the Dog Walker?" I will explain.

Frank lived on West 84th Street with two parrots, three dogs, one snake, and a black widow spider named Samantha. I was sixteen years old when I answered an ad in the back of the *Village Voice* for a dog walker. The day I arrived for the interview Frank greeted me in his underpants with a sledgehammer and both of his parrots on his head (I had interrupted him dismantling the parking-meter heads that he had cut off during the night for the dimes and quarters). As we shook hands I realized a new episode of my life was beginning. For Frank was a con-man hustler far beyond even Bob Semen's imagination. He knew every angle and had a knowledge of off-beat facts like no one I had ever known. In a very serious tone he once asked if I knew that corneas could be sold for three thousand dollars apiece in India. Strangely enough, later in life I would find this to be true. He almost seemed to be considering the idea until brushing it off by jokingly saying that he'd probably sell both of his for a new car that he then wouldn't be able to drive. Contrary to the first impression I may be creating, Frank was a saint. We grew an almost immediate attachment to each other, and for almost two years, no matter how tough things got for him, he somehow always managed to find some work for me to do.

Frank did everything. His flyers read: **"Dog walking, Cat-sitting, House-sitting, Massage, Lose-weight-now—Ask-me-how."** He even advertised for flyer posting. **(THIS FLYER COULD BE YOURS!!!)** I swear I think he just loved hustling. I was walking dogs all day and he was charging the customers six dollars a half-hour, letting me keep five dollars. I'd be running around collecting the dogs, walking them all at the same time. A few times I can remember having as many as ten dogs at once—that was fifty dollars!

On weekend days in the summertime my job was to help illegally sneak cases of beer and soda through the bushes at the West 81st Street entrance to Central Park. We'd bring them to a section of the park known as "the Rambles" and on a good day there, we could make some real money, selling to the hundreds of naked gay men sunbathing and playing games like Parcheesi.

Everything with Frank was an adventure. I think he was my favorite employer ever. I can still hear the sounds of Lionel Richie playing in his house (always), and him excitedly asking if I saw the new video for "Hello," "with the blind lady in it!" I still love Lionel, and in honor of Frank will always take the moment to sing along ("easy like a Sunday mornin'") whenever or wherever that song may come on.

The biggest scam began the second summer I was working for him. It was the summer AIDS was first really being talked about. They used to call it gay cancer at the Rambles. Business was slow in the park, people were sad, but Frank had an idea. Downtown we walked a male corgi named Jake. Jake was a purebred dog and was worth a fortune. Frank saved up almost all his money that summer and bought a female purebred corgi. He named her Miss Lady.

My instructions were to get Jake on an uptown train as quickly as possible to Miss Lady's parlor (Frank's house) and serenade, insinuate, and sometimes even physically aid in their mating. Miss Lady finally got pregnant. She was going to give birth to the first real gold mine at the Frank Valias estate.

At three hundred dollars a puppy, Frank and I had already added up and mentally spent at least half of our soon-to-be fortune. Truly, the financial possibilities of a few male and female thoroughbreds mating and re-mating were endless.

For the last few weeks of Miss Lady's pregnancy, part of my pay and almost all of Frank's income was spent carefully pampering her. On the third week of that September, just as the beer and soda business in the Rambles was coming to an end, Miss Lady gave birth to three absolute mutts. The father, instead of being Jake, the pure breed was CoCo, one of Frank's brought-in runaway German shepherd-beagles from Spanish Harlem.

The disappointment, as always, was almost nonexistent in Frank. I always figured that he either hid it real well or never really believed his dreams were gonna come true anyway. (Nothing bad or, better said, disappointing, ever did seem to faze him.) I asked him about it that afternoon, and he told me a story about how he had served an eleven-year sentence in Attica State Prison.

In the early 1970s Frank had been a 19-year-old gay Puerto Rican kid from 113th Street and Amsterdam Avenue. He had gotten drunk and stayed over at some guy's house. In the middle of the night they had an argument and the guy threw him out into the winter with no clothes on. In his completely obliterated state he kept yelling and banging on the door he had just been thrown from. A few minutes later the guy came out and punched him in his face, breaking his nose. They scuffled with each other for a while, and it ended with Frank sticking him in the stomach with a four-inch blade. He was intoxicated, enraged, and had never been in a fight before in his life. He freaked out, grabbed his clothes, and ran off into the night.

When he got home he told his roommate, who was a nurse, what had happened. After showing him the blade and the spot (right below the belly) where he had stuck the other guy only one time, his roommate said that it probably wasn't as bad as he thought it was.

In the morning, two undercover police officers knocked on his door asking what had happened to his nose, why he had checked into the Lennox Hill Emergency Room the previous night at 3 A.M., and if he knew anything about a stabbing on West End Avenue. Frank came clean and told them the story I have just told you. They asked him to re-explain the part about the stabbing; Frank did so, and then told them how afterwards he blacked out and went home.

Frank was arrested on the spot and later convicted of the murder of his friend, who had been stabbed thirty-seven times. A defense of temporary insanity (that he was intoxicated and physically provoked at the time, and also had been repeatedly molested as a young boy by his father) was barely even attempted or wanted. Frank told me his time in prison was penance. "Eleven long Hail Marys" is what he called them.

I understood a lot more about him from then on. It was no longer a mystery why his always positive spirit and smile somehow seemed to be hiding some faraway sadness.

When Frank finished this story he told me my job that afternoon was to build a new doghouse for his three new guests—Randall, Baby, and Thoroughbred—and to get right back into serenading mode for Tuesday's walk with Jake.

End of Letter to Walt

So now, years later, maybe even lifetimes, if indeed one of you, Frank or Bob, truly are, were . . . you, Walt Whitman, I sit here thinking about our very chance meetings. About how many other of your reincarnations I may have or will come into contact with. And once again, Mr. Whitman, I lay down your supposed masterpiece full of brilliantly colorful *ye's* and rhythmically genius literal vocalizations of greenest pastures and raging seas, for a "not-too-cold-for-January" walk back downtown, and the hope of another chance meeting with you in this lifetime along 8th Avenue.

> *Do not forget to entertain strangers,*
> *for some have entertained angels unawares.*
> Heb. 13: 1–2

SPLITTING WOOD

an incredibly well versed and beautifully (at
all times) drunken man who lived at the Terminal Hotel, whose
dog I used to walk, is responsible for this. At the time, the staying at Terminal Hotel was only a half-step up from being homeless. But this man would save up an extra five dollars a week to
have me walk his dog so that he felt, "Ya know, that way," as
he put it. Unfortunately, this mantra is probably not exact since
I'm writing it from memory.

comb through every religion   furiously turn every stone
quietly wade through every stream

speak to every guru priest deity wise man crazy man ghost
2nd Avenue messiah
believe everything beautiful and good of God no matter how
out there
(i.e. Noah's Ark)
chant every chant   sing every song
meditate levitate eat mushrooms hallucinate or fall into a
trance at the
house of any yogi that will invite you in
(and some that won't)

learn every language of love   dance Hare Krishna
praise Jesus Moses Allah
moan nam myoho rhenge kyo
place flower petals on the Buddha
genuflect past Saint Stanislaus of East 7th Street
confess at your Immaculate Conception church on Ditmars
Boulevard and 29th Street that you always talk about.
recite from the book of Qur'an
take free food or tea from anyone talking about God

and find Heaven,
it's gotta be out there
for there must be God,
and how could any talk of good or God be wrong

RONALD REAGAN,
THE GRIMACE,
AND PUNCTUATION

in an urgent and necessary meeting
between the United States and the Soviet Union about possibly
putting an end to the Nuclear Arms Race War, Press Secretary
Marlin Fitzwater overheard then President Ronald Reagan
explaining to Prime Minister Mikhail Gorbachev a story about a
twelve-hundred-pound man who had slipped, fallen, and gotten
stuck in his own bathroom door.

"This is true story?" asked the puzzled prime minister in his
thick Russian accent. "Yes, yes" answered our very enthusiastic
and obviously absorbed president as he went on with in-depth

facts right down to the exact ankle measurements of this twelve-hundred-pound man.

According to the press secretary who witnessed this, after excusing himself from the table, Mr. Gorbachev was seen moments later frantically waving his arms in utter disarray and confusion toward his interpreter, most likely wondering what the hell Mr. Reagan meant by all this talk of a twelve-hundred-pound man. (Was this some sort of threat or code words?)

I saw it happen again in the "Letters to the Editor" section of a magazine called *The Reader.* A man wrote in asking a two-part question which went as follows . . .

"I know the Hamburgler at McDonalds is supposedly a man, as Mayor McCheese is supposedly a cheeseburger, but what is Grimace? And what does he represent?"

The second part to the question, written by the same person in the same letter, asked, *"What human organs can we live without? And is there a legal market for selling them?"*

Strange questions to be together, I thought. And then I wondered what any of this had to do with the book I'm supposedly writing here about saints. And I guess I understand why the poet Allen Ginsberg, after reading all these stories all bunched up together, answered, when I asked him for a critique of this book you're reading, "I like it a lot, but it seems a bit scattered in thought." And then a few other comments from other people about inconsistency, grammar, and punctuation all seemed valid.

But you know, to defend myself from all this criticism, this life really is scattered and uneven and crazy and upside down. And to be honest it's just too nice a day to sit here any longer thinking about spelling or commas, or even this any longer. Sorry, but it's probably a nice day where you are, too!

P.S. McDonald's had no answer as to the gender, purpose, or meaning of Grimace. And corneas can be sold in India for three thousand dollars (confirmed earlier in life by Frank the Dog Walker).

ADVENTURES IN MALE MODELING AND STREET VENDING

modeling can end you up in some strange places.

I was selling cashews, dried fruits, and fresh-squeezed orange juice for Nick the Eye on the corner of 43rd Street and Lexington Avenue when I was seventeen years old. A guy came up to me and asked if I had modeled before. I said I would if the pay beat this, and this pay was bad. As my father would say, "You sell peanuts, you make peanuts."

He told me his name was Joe Franklel and said to come to his office on West 10th Street. The next day I met him in a room two flights up from a meat-packing company. It smelled like hell.

A bloody meat hell! The wall behind Mr. Franklel's desk was completely filled with eight-by-ten head shots, each individually surrounded with cardboard cut-out gold stars (never a good sign).

I recognized one photo on the wall as the girl in *Saturday Night Fever* who gave all the guys blow jobs. I was very impressed and excited. He said that he would start me out modeling and then we'd slowly break into acting "like they all do." This was starting to sound good.

He handed me what he called a mandatory questionnaire and I told him about my past experience with the scam artist (Bob Semen) who previously had tried to hit me up for some money for head shots. I told him that I was not only broke but hip to that kind of stuff. He assured me it wouldn't cost anything and that I would make a killing with him. I filled out his application, and although some of the questions seemed a bit sexually specific, I could handle that, too.

My first coaching tip from Mr. Franklel was, in his words, "a case scenario reaction." In my words, it was my last coaching tip from Mr. Franklel.

He sat across from me and said: "Now Dito, let's pretend . . . " (Warning to all young street vendors with bigger aspirations: **Beware of this phrase.**)

What would I do, he asked, if, say, I was sent out to meet with a somewhat attractive woman "around forty-ish" who could really hook me up with a modeling job but wanted to have sex with me first. I wasn't sure. He then asked what my reaction would be if she only wanted to see me naked while masturbating. I then asked Mr. Franklel if by any chance he was the forty-ish somewhat attractive woman and left.

Not long after
While selling overpriced cold, wet, and soggy pretzels near West End Park, a man handed me a very flattering pencil sketch

he had just drawn of me holding one of my pretzels. I thanked him as he asked if I had ever sketch-modeled before. The pay was twenty-five dollars an hour, and he could use me for a whole day that weekend. He said his drawings were in the vein of the artist who drew the characters for *Tom of Finland*. I thought, "How harmful can some guy from Finland be?" and agreed.

That Saturday, upon arriving at his studio on Varick Street I was handed a towel, a volume of *Tom of Finland*, and told that I could undress in the bathroom.

Reader . . . have you ever seen a *Tom of Finland* drawing? Imagine John Holmes meets Tom Selleck meets Arnold Schwarzenegger all wrapped up into one (and a lot of them) in a hardcore gay porn. Then imagine you're me, finding this out for the first time in that bathroom, and wondering if selling pretzels is really such a bad job. I thought about it and decided that although I didn't feel I could live up to Tom of Finland's expectations, twenty-five dollars an hour was twenty-five dollars an hour, and selling pretzels was hell.

In my two summers of street vending for everyone from Larry's Fresh Fruit Ices to Chipwich I can't tell you how many of these modeling opportunities had come my way. I mean it seemed incredible how many men out there were willing to pay you just to look at *their* genitals, never mind your own!

A few years later, after actually somehow doing some legitimate modeling jobs, I was sent out on a casting for the designer Fernando Sanchez's runway show. At five-foot-ten I was normally much too short for these types of jobs, but decided to go since I'd been requested.

At the casting, after trying on about fifteen really freaked-out outfits and completely insulting a big model (Iman), simply by not knowing who she was, they said they'd call if they needed me.

At 2 A.M. that night, Fernando Sanchez's assistant called and frantically told me I had to immediately get to their other studio and try on some clothes for a show they were doing the following day. I hopped the train and arrived at this very extravagant penthouse apartment on West 57th Street at around 3 A.M.

Fernando's assistant greeted me completely high out of his mind. He handed me a leather cowboy outfit and hat to put on as he kept running in and out of the room like an insane mouse stopping only to offer me cocaine. I didn't want any.

After about eight changes of clothing in what was starting to seem like a one-man impersonation of The Village People, I was starting to get a little edgy. I mean, the crack mouse was really starting to get me nervous.

He then started offering me things. Now, people on enormous amounts of cocaine can do some pretty strange things, but this was one I had never encountered before. His trip was that he just wanted to give me things—toasters, VCRs, clothes, jewelry, etc. . . . This was a man completely out of control.

He was literally begging me to let him give me whatever he had. He'd then ask me to demand a particular item like a television, and when I did he'd say, "Thank you for letting me give this to you, master, thank you."

After about an hour of this I realized that I was standing in the penthouse apartment of some building on 57th Street loaded down with every household appliance you could imagine, wearing a policeman's outfit and chaps. I must have looked like the winner of an XXX version of "Let's Make A Deal."

The crack mouse, at this point, was beginning to get me really scared. He started asking me, in a fury of cocaine anxiety, if I would allow him to get naked in front of me. When I'd say no he would run out of the room for another fix and return with more presents and ask again. I was trying in my wildest imagination to figure out a way that I could somehow leave this scene alive . . . and with all of my hard-earned prizes. But before I could come up with that answer, in he ran hysterically screaming and naked with cocaine thrown all over his face and chest.

I freaked out and said, "That's it, get the fuck out of my way!" He, with one finger over his mouth, tried a freezed-out cocaine "SHHHHHHHH" as I threw him over a table and ran down twenty-seven flights of stairs like the devil was after me. And I believe the devil was.

About halfway down the block I realized that I had just left all those appliances and jewelry up in that studio. For a minute I entertained the idea of going back for them. Then I thought, "Oh, well," as I put my hands into my new policeman's jacket and pulled out a credit card and some cash that the lunatic had put in there. I ran to a phone and called my friend Jimmy to come meet me at one of the guitar stores on 48th Street just as they would be opening. And in the background of my 6 A.M. phone call to Jimmy, while watching all of the early street vendors on their way to their corners, amid the herd of old men pushing their frankfurter carts I noticed a kid who looked around four years younger than me with that God-I-hate-getting-up-this-early look on his face that I used to have. So I bought a Frozade off him . . .

on Mr. Sanchez of course.

Some things change, some things stay the same.

FINDING ENLIGHTENMENT THROUGH TALK SHOW HOST RICHARD BAY

in a near-death fetal position at St. Vincent's Hospital, in October, while withdrawing from everything (again), through scattered unclear mutter just as visiting hours were up and I began to leave, Jimmy took hold of my hand and faintly (as always) gasped out, "I wouldn't want to see a spaceship without you." I looked at him, pulled up a chair, and decided to stay until they threw me out.

I sat there thinking about how my father used to look at any cut or bruise I ever had and say, "You'll live." I thought about an interview with Dion and the Belmonts that's been my greatest inspiration in writing ever since Jimmy gave me a "The

Wanderer" 45 rpm as a Christmas gift. In it, the interviewer asked Dion why, if he really was from such a tough neighborhood and grew up with so much violence, did he write almost entirely about love and broken hearts in such a comforting and sometimes even sappy way. His answer was that when you grow up with it and you really know what's up, if you get real lucky, and try real hard, you can sometimes end up with a whole different sort of understanding.

And somehow, among all of these serene thoughts and words and quotes that have stayed and will stay with me, a vision of Richard Bay being interviewed on "Live at Five" appeared almost angelic-like over Jimmy's hospital bed on the TV. I'm sorry if I'm killing the moment or mood here with this but it's true. Richard Bay, the permanently suntanned N.Y.C. WOR-TV Channel 9 low-budgeted emperor of trash-TV talk shows (pre–Jerry Springer) was being interviewed in a piece I had already seen a week earlier. When asked if there were any drawbacks to his newly found fame, his answer was simply, "Only one. That every night I have to go to sleep, and when I do, I can't wait to see the next morning." It was something Jimmy would say whenever things were good.

And with that it seemed Jimmy finally went to sleep. So while the nurses overlooked me staying late past visiting hours I grabbed a blanket to rest in my chair, knowing the watchful eye of Saint Richard was there over both of us, and nothing tonight could go too wrong.

CHERRY VANILLA

i got a phone call one day from a raspy sexy womanly Ruth Young jazz voice. She told me she was a friend of photographer Bruce Weber and that they were both interested in coming to check out my band. She said they had been looking at a picture he had taken of me one afternoon down on Watts Street and were thinking about doing an article on my band for this big hip New York magazine. I asked her to please put my friend Ray on the phone, since I get at least one of these types of pranks from him every day. She told me she was for real, laughed, and said she didn't even know Ray. Half-believing her, I said that my band was playing on Friday at this little dive on 1st Avenue called the Lismar Lounge and that if she told me her name I'd put her on our guest list. "OK, sure, great, just put Cherry Vanilla on, plus two." Cherry Vanilla! "Would you like another cup of coffee?" I said, imitating her two-pack-a-day voice. I had just been listening to this Roger Waters Pink Floyd album called *The Pros and Cons of Hitchhiking*, and Cherry Vanilla was one of the voice characters on the record. She played a waitress, and that was one of her lines. "Oh God, do you really have that album!?" she said laughing out loud, and I knew right away it really was her.

That Friday, for the entire night all I could think about was meeting Cherry Vanilla. After the show, the most attractive forty-year-old, jet-red-headed crazy I had ever met came over to me all excited and smiling. It was that voice again. "Man, that was out of this world! It's beautiful outside. We should all go for a walk, smoke some tea, and get some drinks." We all went out, got drunk and high together, and wandered all the way down to this one great pier on the West Highway where we sang songs, laughed, and danced for hours under the magnificent blue lights. After going over to Cherry's 2nd Avenue apartment at around 4 A.M., I knew the night had either come to its absolute climax or complete finish when I ended up getting stuck upside down and drunk in this weird reverse sit-up machine she used to spin around in after getting high.

Over the next few years we became very good friends. We'd usually see each other at least once a month. The only thing that you could be sure of when you got a call from Cherry was that you'd be in for a great circus-type dinner or party event. She'd have me meet her in wild little hidden incense-ridden Tibetan meditation houses on backstreets in Chinatown or at the off-off-off-Broadway Theater of the Ridiculous that was started by a friend of hers back in the Andy Warhol days. Or maybe just meet in some quiet little teahouse on the Lower East Side. When you'd show up, she'd be there, always terribly excited to see you. She'd have a drink in one hand, a transvestite in the other, and someone like Chet Baker, Deborah Harry, or Angela Bowie at her side. They'd be screaming about getting high in the rain forest with Salvador Dali, or maybe if you got lucky, she'd tell you about drinking at the Copacabana with Tony Bennett and Frank Sinatra when she was a kid. She'd tell me stories about traveling through Europe on a bus in the mid-'70s with The Sex Pistols, The Clash, and her band, which consisted of Sting and Steward Copeland as backup musicians. She'd talk about hanging out in New York back in the days of Max's Kansas City and The Factory with Andy Warhol, who had changed her name from Kathleen Doherty to Cherry Vanilla because of her fire-red hair. Cherry had more stories in her than anyone I ever met. Her stories made me dream. They would have made anyone dream. They were funny and sad and wild and all true.

She would take me around and introduce me to people like Johnny Thunders or Jane County and tell them that they were meeting the next big star. She put my picture on the People Page of the *Daily News* right there next to Zsa Zsa Gabor and Bruce Willis and told at least half a million Midwestern housewives, through supermarket tabloids and magazines, that my music was so good "the world would soon take me away." She made me believe that it all somehow could possibly happen.

I remember her and another friend of mine, Michael Alago, bringing me to a party once for Liza Minnelli. When we walked in, Liza Minnelli, to whom they had once before introduced me, came up to me, remembered my name, and thanked *me* for coming. I was in shock and trying very hard not to let her, or anyone, know just how freaked out I was. Mrs. Minnelli (that sounds weird), Liza, whatever, then introduced me to her friends: Gregory, Bobby, Harvey, and Christopher. When I turned around to shake their heads, I mean hands, it was Gregory Peck, (Bobby) DeNiro, Harvey Keitel, and Christopher Walken. It was like meeting some kind of living Mount Rushmore. When you meet people like that, whom you've seen for so many years on television and in the movies, they almost don't even look real. To me it looked like the *Deer Hunter*, *Taxi Driver*, and *To Kill a Mockingbird* were all on TV at the party. And for lack of a better greeting I chose three "Holy cows" and one "Holy shit" while shaking each of their hands, and when I say each of their hands I mean all eight of them. After telling a quite uninterested Christopher Walken that I was from his hometown, Astoria, Queens, I went immediately to the bar and had three kamikazes. Before the end of the night I found myself dancing with Sylvia Miles, trying to pick up Bianca Jagger, and then in desperate intoxication telling Liza Minnelli how I cried my eyes out over her mother, Judy Garland's, performance of "Somewhere over the Rainbow" on some old TV show that she looked drunk on.

At Liza Minnelli's wedding anniversary. From left: Giancarlo Esposito, Liza Minnelli, Me, Lisa Marie, Michael Alago, Phil from Monster Magnet, unknown party goer

Cherry, of course, even though it was probably her thousandth party like this, was every bit as excited and starstruck as me. From across the floor I could see her dancing up a storm and moving in on all the famous eligible bachelors. But she was always like that. Excited about everything. Excited about life. She'd be dancing that way at a party on Astoria Boulevard!

The last time I saw Cherry was when I was leaving New York for my first real tour with my band. She seemed kind of sad. She was pretty broke at the time and had taken on some ratty job at a racetrack in Connecticut taking bets on jai-alai and telling uninterested tourists where the hot spots in New York City are (sending unsuspecting white-collar conservative families on vacation to NY drag bars). When I asked her how she was doing, in her always poetic way she said, "Oh, you know honey, it's real tough out there, money, everything, but hey this is the path we've chosen."

We spent the entire night at a little place in the West Village called Tea and Sympathy. We sat, as usual, in a dark, half-lit corner drinking lemon tea and wine. I had a slice of really good coconut custard pie. A magazine had asked her to interview me and was paying the check. An interview with *me*? What could I tell her? We tried it for about five minutes but then gave up. After a few more drinks and two more slices of that pie (it was really good), she walked me to my tour bus on 17th Street. Around 1 A.M., as we walked past Gansevoort Street (beautiful Gansevoort Street) we saw a woman sitting outside, selling a bunch of stuffed animals and clothes and books. We stopped and looked around. All of a sudden Cherry got all excited, and in her always over-the-top beautiful kind of way said, "*The Prophet*! Have you ever read this book?" I said no. She asked how much it was, paid three dollars for it, and said that no one should ever buy this book for themselves, that it had to be bought for you. She gave it to me and we said good-bye.

I'm somewhere on the road I think in New Jersey now. The sun is starting to come up. I know I'm getting pretty far from home because it's been at least three hours since I could even faintly see the Empire State Building. I haven't slept yet. I think I'm kind of nervous. I'm about three-quarters of the way through *The Prophet* and I can't stop reading it. It's beautiful. I'm thinking about the first time Cherry told me it would all work out. I'm thinking about how she believed in me and how she made me believe in myself. I'm wondering how many people in the past she's made feel this way. I've got Van Morrison on in the back of the bus, "Tir Na Nog, Eternal Youth." He's singing about going way way back. About happiness from within. Cherry always said his voice was healing. She said it made you feel like someone was out there. She always made me feel like someone was out there. I'm thinking about last night on Gansevoort Street, and *The Prophet*, and about how things like that just seem to happen when you're around Cherry Vanilla.

124

Parts of the interview we were supposed to have had at Tea and Sympathy later became this article:

It was 1988. I'd spent
most of '86 & '87 hanging out
with jazz musicians. I was
feeling a little old for rock and
roll. I first saw heard and fell in
love with them on a bitter cold
night on 1st Avenue.

I did drunk aerobics to
their demos and told everyone I
could about them. They kept me
up. They kept me young. They

kept me dreamin'.
Old groupies never die,
they just become celibate and
switch to fairy-godmother mode!
Well, like another great
rock & roller once said, and like
your dear old Aunty Cherry
keeps repeating, "This is the trip.
This is the best part of the trip."
It's gonna be wild. It's gonna be
great. You're gonna be stars. But
dig it. We are never, ever gonna
be this young again.
—Cherry Vanilla

a guide to recognizing your saint

CHRISTMAS IN
NEW YORK WITH
ANNETTE

i met her in virginia beach at a club called
The Boathouse. I was on the road with my band opening up for
the Stray Cats. She came backstage with a couple of friends of
mine from New York. She had long, red, fire-red hair, milky
white smooth skin, and the bluest eyes I had ever seen. I almost
fell drop dead right there. I never really believed in it but I was
in love and I didn't even know her name.

I'd been on the road for about a month and I was freaking
out. Lisa in New York wasn't talking to me. She had met Woody
Allen and gotten a small part in his latest movie, *Alice,* and I
imagine Astoria was feeling a million miles away from

Hollywood to her. I was out of my mind. I couldn't eat, couldn't sleep, she wasn't taking my calls, I was feeling nowhere. It had gotten so bad that two nights earlier in Cleveland I just walked right off stage in the middle of the set. I remember taking a walk that night with my bass player Eric to some strip joint in this area called the Flats. I asked him the forever questions of the brokenhearted, "How long will I feel this way? What do I do to make it better? How do I do it?" That night and for the rest of the week I couldn't be alone. I couldn't sit still. If Eric, Johnny, or anyone for that matter were going anywhere, I'd go.

"The supermarket, oh I'll come."

As soon as I would get there I would want to leave. I would have to leave! I'm sure you know the feeling.

When I met Annette everything changed. All I could think of was her. She was the sweetest girl I had ever met. She was an angel and I somehow envisioned that God had sent her to me to make things better.

After our show in Virginia I took her out to see our tour bus. We had the band Kiss's tour bus and it was wild. We all had our own bunks with VCRs, TVs, and video games (Tetris). In the front was a living room with a giant neon sign that read, "Hotel California," and in the back was our kitchen with a microwave, refrigerator, everything. She must have thought I was some big rock star at the time. I probably did as well.

We had two days off in Virginia. I spent them with her. We went to the beach, the scary houses, the arcades, the bumper cars, everywhere. She was fun and I was falling in love. The last night that we were together I remember lying next to her in my hotel bed and her whispering in my ear with her Southern accent, "You missin' somebody?" I answered "No" and realized at that moment, for the first time in my life, that I really wasn't missing anybody or anything and I was in love.

I had to leave the next morning and go out on the road again. She had already left to go to work. I called her there to say good-bye but didn't feel like it was enough. I remember thinking if I could just stay a little longer or bring her to New York I know I could make her mine.

When we were pulling out I talked our bus driver Billy into driving by the store where she worked. When we pulled up I was running crazy through the bus looking for some kind of present or anything I could give her to let her know what she meant to me. Barbara, our sax player, gave me some flowers and I put them in a box along with a tape of Chet Baker singing *Blame It on My Youth*. I ran into the store and gave them to Annette. She laughed and kissed me.

I sent her postcards from everywhere in America. I called her from late-night truck stops, and two months later she came to visit me back home in New York. It was her first time here. I took her everywhere. We ate on Mulberry Street, went on the rowboats in Central Park, walked around Saint Mark's Place and watched the ball drop on 42nd Street. I wanted to keep her so bad.

It's been six months now and I'm on an Amtrak train somewhere between Maryland and D.C. I'm on my way back to New York after visiting her. I'm looking out at some cows and horses and grass everywhere. I'm thinking about how in life things come and go.

Last night we rented Woody Allen's *Manhattan*. So many things in it really hit home for us. I'm thinking about that one last scene where Woody Allen is running down 7th Avenue desperately trying to get to Mariel Hemingway. I'm thinking about when she tells him that he has to have a little more faith in people. I'm thinking about a million things. But to be honest, all I'm really thinking about is Annette and how much I want her.

Just before I left we decided that in December, after this semester of school, she would come live with me in New York. I know how things can change though, they often do. And although it's the middle of August, and I know that when I get back all the fire hydrants on my corner will be spraying all of the little Puerto Rican Indios under that blazing hot New York heat wave I've been hearing so much about, all I can think of is Christmas in New York with Annette.

Annette with Duckman

ONE NIGHT

i thought she was sleeping until I heard her call out from across the room, "Will you bring me a glass of water?" I did. Then in her always-sleepy tone and drawl she said, "Do you remember when you were a little boy and you would ask your mama to bring you a glass of water?" Yeah. "You know half the time you weren't even thirsty. You just wanted that hand that was attached to that glass that was attached to that person you just wanted to stay there until you fell asleep." She took the glass of water that I brought her and just sat it down full on the table next to her. Wow, I thought. What am I gonna do with love like this.

BRUCE WEBER

"hi, ah, dito, it's ah, bruce." Try it again, but
more baritone, more raspy. "Hi, ah, Dito, it's ah, Bruce." Not so
cigarette sounding. Lighter, kind of Marlon Brando's Godfather,
but nicer.

Bruce Weber is a photographer who over the years has
been a sort of overlooking guardian angel to me and my band.
That opening telephone conversation ("Hi, ah, Dito, it's ah,
Bruce") line has been followed by everything from, "I'm here
with Robert Mitchum, and if it's all right with you I'd like to
record a quick conversation between him and your girlfriend
right now for my new movie," to, "Do you think maybe you and

your band could come down to make some karate fight 'ooh' and 'ahh' sounds for this short Jean-Claude Van Damme movie today?" Or it could be, "If you have nothing to do this weekend I'd love to fly you up to my place in the Adirondacks to sing "Happy Birthday" for my girlfriend Nan."

Then there was the time he couldn't get the rights to the original introduction to the song "My Funny Valentine" by the great jazz player Gerry Mulligan and wanted to know if I would come fill in and do it for Chet Baker. "Don't change your hair for me, not if you care for me, stay little valentine stay." One night he had a vision of me singing old standards just like Tony Bennett and decided to make a movie letting me play that part.

I met Bruce when I was nineteen years old. I was boxing at a gym on 30th Street and 8th Avenue called Father and Sons. A friend of mine had told me to go over to this place on 56th Street called Click Modeling Agency. He said that a couple of other guys from the gym had gone there and made a lot of money having their pictures taken, and that some of them even ended up in magazines. I had spent about half my life as a kid jumping in front of "live" news cameras anytime any kind of crime had been committed in my neighborhood, and had one brief moment about an hour into a movie called *Tempest* where me, Giuseppi, Graziano, and Tommy Byrnes can be seen (after sneaking in) walking by as extras with all our middle fingers sticking out. Well, for these reasons, along with me being broke, it sounded like a pretty good idea.

All I had to do was go on Wednesday at twelve noon to 56th Street and 7th Avenue and bring some pictures. On my way over, I stopped at Playland on 49th Street and got two strips of four pictures in their one-dollar photo booth. I felt kind of embarrassed going into the booth alone, but every other picture I had of myself included at least five or six other crazies making faces or holding up beers and I needed some pictures of me alone.

When I got to Click Modeling Agency there was a row of about two hundred of the most beautiful girls I had ever seen, and about fifty guys that looked like they had just walked out of a Sears and Roebuck's catalogue. I got on line for about twenty minutes. When I finally got near the front there was a big sign that read, "If you are a guy and under six feet tall, you don't belong here!" I knew there was something weird about these people. You see, I grew up in a very Greek and Italian neighborhood. I was actually considered kind of tall there. But now I was among this sea of perfect giants, trying to figure out if it would be more embarrassing to get to the front, pushing five-foot-ten with my combat boots, holding eight pictures from a Playland video-arcade photo booth, and get turned down, or just get off right there and walk back past the two hundred beautiful girls I had been hitting on for the past twenty minutes.

I stayed on line and when I got to the front I met a guy named John Giambrone. John looked like a crazy evil villain from a science fiction comic book. When I showed him my pictures he laughed and told me that there was a photographer named Bruce Weber, who at the time was doing a lot of things with boxers and might be interested in meeting me. John made a call and hooked it up that I would meet Bruce the next day at his studio on Watts Street.

When I got home that night the first thing I did was tell my girlfriend, who at the time pretty much lived for each new issue of *Vogue*. When I said I was going to meet Bruce Weber she freaked out and told me that he was her favorite photographer in the world. Before long she'd made me a nervous wreck. We immediately called Tommy Byrnes (my co-star fellow snuck-in extra in *Tempest*). Tommy worked at a tuxedo rental place and was the guy with the clothes. In case of emergencies such as funerals, weddings, and now meeting Bruce Weber, Tommy was the man to call. Next up was Frankie Rock. Frankie was a sort of Latin punk-rock Desi Arnaz hairdresser with a Sylvester

Stallone voice, whose only ambition in life besides being a rock star was to either marry a model or some rich old lady he might someday meet at the salon:

"The chemicals I gotta put in these viejas' hair is murder on the hands!"

I arrived at Bruce's studio the next day with seven bald spots from Frankie, and a thirteen-year-old's communion suit since Tommy didn't have enough notice to come up with a decent outfit. I'd decided that because it was summer out I'd probably look better wearing my Guinea-T undershirt rather than a mustard-stained, three-sizes-too-small Communion jacket. When Bruce came out to meet me wearing a flannel shirt and a bandanna on his head I can't tell you how relieved I was.

We hung out for a while and he took some pictures. I must have told him at least three dozen nervous stories about Antonio in jail, Frankie's haircuts, and my band, while he just clicked away smiling and laughing at all my nervous nonsense. He made it real easy, and I don't ever remember enjoying having my picture taken as much without being drunk.

Two months later, one of the pictures he had taken of me came out in a big New York magazine called *Details*. It was the first time I had ever legitimately been in a magazine. It took up a full page and right under it was that write-up about my band by Cherry Vanilla. I must have bought at least twenty issues that month. I gave copies out to everyone from my father to my old manager Bob Semen, who immediately framed it and stuck it in the window of that Playland arcade window along with his telephone number printed across the bottom.

Right after that things started going real great for my band. We were in everything from *Interview* to *Vanity Fair* to a ten-page layout in a magazine called *Splash,* and all we had to do was hang out with a bunch of beautiful girls. It was all happening and finally hit home with a write-up on the People Page of the *Daily News. Vanity Fair, Details,* and the

New Yorker are one thing, but the *Daily News* is what your father believes.

Not too much later we signed a deal with Geffen Records while we were out on the road. When we returned home, since we hadn't yet received our money advances, we went back to our old jobs. I was working on the West Side docks of Manhattan unloading trucks, Barbara was making burritos on 17th Street, Johnny was roofing, and Danny and Eric were painting. One week later the phone rang. "Hi, ah, Dito, it's ah, Bruce." (I knew it was going to be a good day.) "I was wondering if you guys would mind coming down to Miami for a week to do a Gianni Versace clothing ad? It will pay you three thousand dollars each plus airfare and hotels; the only problem is that you'll have to come out a few days early to get a tan on the beach for the pictures." "Bruce, and I'm not kidding," I replied, "if you want us to walk there we'll leave now." He laughed and booked it for the next day.

The people at Geffen Records didn't think it was a very good idea that we model for clothes. They were afraid that people would get the wrong image of us. Five tanned drunks called them two days later from Miami to tell them they didn't care.

We stayed in a first-class hotel and had three separate rooms that all connected. They each had liquor and food cabinets that would be re-stocked every night. For the entire time we were in Miami, at pretty much any hour, you could find at least fifteen drunken models all lying around our rooms. On the shoot was a guy named Carlos who was from the area and would take us around to all the local strip joints and cool hangouts that no one else knew about. One night while we were flying drunk down these dirt roads somewhere in an area called Little Haiti we ended up at a voodoo-looking bar that had about twenty stray dogs walking around in it. Our nights were as wild as our days, which were spent being photographed by Bruce, singing along half-dazed and dreamy to the sounds of Tony Bennett while dancing with beautiful Talisa and an army of other drop-dead knockout girls. We were getting two haircuts a day, wearing three-thousand-dollar suits, and actually getting paid for it!

On our last night there, Bruce threw a wrap-up party for everyone on a place called Star Island. Star Island was an exclusive island whose residents included Bob Hope, Julio Iglesias, Don Johnson, Melanie Griffith, and a few other celebrities. Bruce asked if we would play at the party, and rented us some guitars and amplifiers.

Star Island was one of the most beautiful places I had ever seen. To get there we had to drive across a long, narrow bridge where we were cleared to enter by a dozen guards. The area where the party was taking place looked like a Hawaiian set right out of an old Elvis movie. There were hula dancers everywhere; torches were burning; pigs were roasting. It was a dream.

Around midnight we went on to play. There was a giant unforgettable mustard-yellow moon right over our heads covering all of Miami. I expected to see Elizabeth Taylor and Montgomery Clift out there among the crowd, falling in love right there in front of us at this perfect moment. After playing for about forty-five minutes in one of the most happy, intoxicated states of my life to an audience of the very same nature, we put down our instruments for a dive into the ocean.

Barbara fit the charred remains of the roasted pig head over mine as I attempted to make out with the designer Patricia Field by telling her I loved her Betsey Johnson stores. She would have no part in it.

Heavy drinking for me has always led to public nudity. That being the case, Barbara and I got high naked and dove off the edge of the island with the rest of the band. The roasted pig (with apple in mouth) joined us in our fun as a sort of mascot, life preserver, conversation piece, and off-beat beach ball. As we swam around I can remember looking up at the sky and thinking how perfect everything felt. I was thinking about how I was going to tell Bruce what a good friend he had always been to us. I was thinking about how I was going to thank him for everything. And it wasn't because of all the materialistic or glamorous sides to it. It was just the way he had always done things with us like it was no big deal, like we deserved it. It was the way he would ask if we "minded" going to Florida or would "do him a favor" and come down to have our pictures taken with him.

As I was enjoying the beauty of the moment thinking all these great dreamy thoughts and trying to figure out what our friend John Hubba was screaming out to us from the island, Barbara broke the tranquility by relaying John's message that we were swimming in shark-infested waters naked with the

photo: Bruce Weber

Gianni Versace ad with Gutterboy that will "run nowhere never!" said Mr. Versace in an angry Italian accent. "They look like three blind, drunk mice!"

sweet scent of freshly roasted pig. I got out of that water in about two seconds, and to this day still fear the ocean, mustard-lit moons, and a terrible recurring dream of drowning pigs clinging tightly to me. This all with no damage done to the memory of Star Island.

Woody Allen once said that the reason we try so hard to make things perfect in art is because in life they so seldom are. Both art and life on that trip were perfect. So when I look at a real dreamy Bruce Weber photo now with some new up-and-coming model sucking in their cheekbones, I don't think about how nice the picture is. The only thing I think about is how much fun they must have had taking it.

138

atilla was a famous male model when I was seventeen years old. I know this because Lari Anne was in love with him, and I was in love with Lari Anne. She would show me pictures of him in *Vogue* with his long beautiful curly hair and then, seeing my not-very-well-hidden jealousy, kiss my always shaved head and in a loving consolation sort of way say, "But I'm with you."

When I wasn't jealous of Atilla things were great. I disappeared in love downtown with her for two years. We hung out at CBGB's, The Mudd Club, Irving Plaza, Rat Cage, the A7, the 2+2, and all the other freaked-out hidden New York hard-core hangouts. I was a skinhead and she had a crew cut and wore Catholic-school miniskirts.

I met Lari Anne on a New Year's Eve. She, her sister Arianna, and all the rest of her under-five-foot-two female Latina gang of beauties wanted to hang out with my punk band, Major Conflict, for the night.

We drank Tango and Old English at Johnny Waste's house in the Ravenswood Projects all night long. Ray, one of my best friends, lost his virginity that night on the roof with one of them as everyone else tried to kick in the roof door, interrupting his initiation into manhood.

Billy, Johnny Waste, Andy Apathy, and all the others were out of control while I spent most of the night just staring into the mirror, in some romantic Tango high, at Lari Anne's most beautiful Mexican-with-Italian-mobster-father's blue eyes.

photo: Vinny Lotito

Major Conflict at CBGB's

There was a roaming outlaw hard-core party that night at Coney Island. Minor Threat was blasting on ten through junked-out speakers in Nick's angel-dust fogged-out Pacer. Everyone's crammed in this New Year's Eve, flying eighty-eighty-five-ninety through Queens, Manhattan, Brooklyn. Giant snowflakes are everywhere as me and Lari Anne make out the whole way there.

I fell seventeen-year-old in love. And you tell me what could be more strong. At seventeen nothing is rational, nothing needs to make sense, nothing needs to be planned. At seventeen love is not love, love is crazy love and I fell crazy in love with Lari Anne.

I used to cut out of school when she would stay home sick. I'd take the 7 train out to Main Street, Flushing, and catch the Q19A bus to her house in Whitestone. After her parents would go out she'd sneak me up and I swear we'd have sex for hours and hours. Seventeen-year-old sex. You know, you come in a minute and then you do it again and again. I swear I think we'd just keep doing it to see how many times I could come.

Seventeen is a funny age, though. At seventeen I believe you can actually have sex for a whole day without the girl obtaining any pleasure at all, and the best part about it is that at that age you really couldn't give a damn:

"What do you mean you didn't come, I'm breakin' freakin' records here."

I was crazy for Lari Anne. She used to tell me about Jack Kerouac and Allen Ginsberg. She knew about all these real weird people like Bruce Weber and Andy Warhol, and she'd buy just about every fashion magazine in the world. I had no idea who any of these people were, but at the time found them all intimidating and for some weird reason believed them all to be French, especially after her explaining that the Kerouac book she was reading, *Tristessa,* meant "sadness" in French.

Aside from Atilla, Bruce Weber was probably at the top of that list. You see of course whenever she'd talk about any of those fashion model, French, or poet people I'd always act completely uninterested. And as soon as she'd leave the room I'd immediately go right through every last magazine and book she had like a nosy old grandmother. I'd see that damn Bruce Weber's name, and I wasn't sure which guy he was in the

Gutterboy

Dito. 21. Writer, lead singer, guitarist of Gutterboy. Queens kid, Astoria. Shy typa guy. Arms and the inner light. Nicaraguan father, Irish mother. "She took off around two years ago." He has no idea where she is now. "She called me up on Christmas and said, 'What's happening?' I said 'Wow Ma, where ya been?'"

I ask him if he ever read Kerouac. "Man, *On the Road*, that last chapter. It's so real. To me anyway. That's the way it really is." I love him. Wanna hold him. Keep him secret, safe. Not let the world take him away. But his music's so good, I know it will.

Oh well, that's cool. At least my life's been saved once again by rock 'n' roll.

Gutterboy will be appearing in New York City on March 25th at the Lismar Lounge, 41 First Avenue.
—Cherry Vanilla

photographed by Bruce Weber

photographed by Bruce Weber

photo: Bruce Weber

EDITED BY ALAN WELTZ **DETAILS**

Suddenly, this Section

For *Details* magazine

picture but whichever one it was, he sure did look a lot better than me. I even saw his name next to Atilla once, and the fact that they hung out made everything worse.

Soho was one of our favorite places to go. Lari Anne always dragged me to the Thalia Theater on some backstreet to see old foreign movies. I liked *Los Olvidados,* but most of them drove me nuts. I always wondered why it was that if John Candy slipped and fell on a banana peel it was idiotic, but if some French guy did, it was genius. I actually got thrown out of the Thalia once during a screening of *Betty Blue* for arguing with the entire audience this very same point.

On Sunday afternoons we'd go to the hard-core matinees at CBGB's with everybody slam-dancing and diving off the stage to bands like Reagan Youth, Bad Brains, Urban Waste, The Mob, The Young and The Useless, Agnostic Front, and The Nihilistics. I remember doing a show with the UK Subs at The Rock Hotel while the place was being torn apart during one of our songs. The pile-up on stage, on top of me, had gotten so high that I lost my guitar. When I finally crawled out from under I could hear someone banging on it with horrible out-of-tune chords and feedback just exploding my speakers. I followed my guitar chord to Lari Anne who was just banging away completely into it and out of it. I loved that. I loved her.

Years later, after not seeing her for a long time, I thought of her during that first *Details* magazine interview about my new band, Gutterboy. The interviewer was Cherry Vanilla, the photographer was Bruce Weber, and in the interview, when out of nowhere Cherry asked me about Jack Kerouac, I told her that she had to promise that in the article she would mention how my old girlfriend Lari Anne had told me about all the people involved in it before I even knew who any of them were, and about how I used to just burn up about them. She laughed and promised.

The editor cut that part of the interview out and there I was in the April issue of a big fashion magazine, photographed by my high school enemy Bruce Weber, interviewed by a member of Andy Warhol's Factory, and talking all knowledgeable about my good friend Jack Kerouac.

I ran into one of Lari Anne's under-five-foot-two Latina crew, Patti Joseph, on an N train going downtown not too long after the magazine came out. The first thing she said was that Lari had told her if she ever ran into me to tell me (in her very sarcastic manner) to say "Hi" to Jack and Bruce for her. She told me Lari had gotten married and moved to France. How ironic, I thought, as I left beautiful little Patti at the West 49th Street station on my way to the Ziegfeld Theater to meet a friend for the opening of John Candy's new movie, *Uncle Buck*.

When I miss being seventeen, which is not often, I miss being seventeen with you, Lari Anne.

P.S. I also later heard Atilla (the model) was gay . . . ("too bard" as Lari Anne's strong-Mexican-accented Abuelita would say).

144

ALLEN GINSBERG WANTS BITTER MELON, BUT NO GENITALIA

allen ginsberg, in his very scholarly but always completely puzzled voice, invited me and my band into his apartment on East 12th Street for tea and an egg. I liked him the minute we met. He reminded me a lot of my father, with his very casual short-sleeve white shirt, glasses and pencil in top right pocket, very down-to-earth way of talking, and his messy little kitchen on the Lower East Side of Manhattan. It was October.

We had gone to Mr. Ginsberg's place to take some pictures with him for our new album cover. As we followed him into his kitchen he muttered kind of to himself, or maybe us, something about relaxing first and talking over eggs and tea later. He was very nice, but preoccupied in a strange way. We all sat at the table as he went on talking, always half to himself, and half to us, about Taoism and Buddhism, while eating his hard-boiled egg along with its **shell.** He asked a lot of questions. I was surprised at how interested he was in our thoughts. Through all the talk of religion, Buddha, and the afterlife, the only question I was really interested in finding the answer to was whether or not he knew that he had just eaten the entire shell along with his egg. He and my guitar player, Danny, immediately hit it off. Danny was a big fan of Mr. Ginsberg's and was real hip to all of that spiritual stuff. I, on the other hand, besides my concern about the egg incident, was preoccupied with trying to figure out if Taoism was a religion, a card game, or something else.

After some eggs (shelled, thank you), tea, and fascinating talk, Mr. Ginsberg said that he wanted to take some pictures of us sitting right where we were. I was expecting him to pull out some really cool old '50s camera, or maybe some new expensive one. Instead what he pulled out was this junky-looking four-year-old disposable-type family Kodak. He clenched it tightly with both hands and told us not to move. This very concerned and hardworking confused look all of a sudden took over his face as he asked if we knew how to load the film for the other camera he had or if he should just stay with the disposable. "These little ones really do take nice pictures, though. Yes, we'll just stay with this one." We were now sure that he was, without question, the right photographer for Gutterboy.

The day was full of quiet muttered outbursts from Mr. Ginsberg, such as, "Most information, least syllables" followed usually by small inside laughter. There were stories of drugs with William Burroughs, Jack Kerouac, and even the Dalai Lama, followed in mid-sentence by anything from Tibetan chants (Gate Gate Paragate Parasamgate), to mutterings on his fears of death and all in one afternoon. He had a unique way of seeming completely confused and distraught and lost, but at the same time, completely on. It was like he was always talking half to himself and half to this third party that only he knew about without ever seeming to ignore or miss anything you would say.

We took pictures in his kitchen, in his bathroom, out on the fire escape, on his roof, everywhere. We were drinking and smoking the entire time and by the end of the day we were completely gone. I told Mr. Ginsberg, in complete high lunacy, that I thought we should go over to Macy's on 34th Street and take naked pictures until the police arrested all of us. He hesitated and mumbled something like, "Well that would be kind of interesting," with his kind of puzzled inside laugh. After a five-minute almost completely, I'm sure, thought-filled mental hiatus, almost as if he broke out of some trance, he turned and said to me (after I had completely forgotten about my idea about the Macy's photos), "Well you know the naked idea at Macy's might just attract a little too much attention, but we could try that here if you want."

We were high out of our heads and before we knew it all five of us were completely naked sitting around his room. Mr. Ginsberg lit some candles by his living room shrine, and put on some "mood music" just right for the occasion. It was a song called "Everybody Is a Little Homosexual" from an old record of songs he had recorded years earlier. He set his camera up in his complicated way, got ready to take our picture, and then stopped for a second to tell us that for the record company the pictures probably "will be a little more useful if there is no genitalia showing." We agreed, and went on to take our ungenitalia'd naked pictures with Allen Ginsberg. Right about this time two people from the art department of the record company came by to see how our photo shoot was going. As we lay high and naked over a Buddhist shrine in Mr. Ginsberg's bedroom, they decided to stop it there. We felt we had probably taken enough pictures anyway and got ready to leave.

From there we were going over to visit Bruce Weber about some pictures he had taken of us. Since Allen Ginsberg and Bruce Weber were mutual fans of each other we asked Mr. Ginsberg if he'd like to come along. We called Bruce to tell him Allen Ginsberg was coming along and he was delighted. When we arrived at Bruce's place on Watts Street the first thing I remember is Mr. Ginsberg asking Bruce if he knew a good cheap place to develop film. Bruce told him he usually sent it out to a lab on 23rd Street to be developed. Mr. Ginsberg told him he dropped his off at a twenty-four-hour Kodak on Avenue A.

Me, Bruce, and Mr. Ginsberg then went up to see Bruce's personal collection of photos in one of his private studios. There were, of course, quite a few photographs of some pretty incredible-looking naked guys, undoubtedly capturing Mr. Ginsberg's eye. In his always inquisitive and straightforward manner he asked Bruce, "So, uh, Mr. Weber, you have photographed some pretty good-looking young men here. May I ask you what gender you are?" Inquiring in Allen Ginsberg's language if Bruce was gay. I almost fell over as that's kind of an unasked question with Bruce for some reason. In an awkward sort of way he hesitantly answered, "Well, Allen, I just kind of photograph whatever I'm feeling on a particular day." Mr. Ginsberg, quick and humorous as always, replied, "Well I guess you sure must feel like photographing naked men a lot."

Bruce seemed constantly entertained by Ginsberg's strangeness, while Ginsberg was pretty much preoccupied with trying to figure out, "What this strange little thing I got on St. Mark's Place for a buck is? I mean it gives me a big light whenever I do this (he, in his very out-of-nowhere way, demonstrates), but I can't seem to connect it to anything." Bruce explained that it was a light meter and that it wasn't supposed to be attached to a camera. "Well at least I get a (demonstrates) flash out of it," Ginsberg said, followed by a, "Wow! That was a big one." It was a bizarre meeting to say the least. When we left I remember

Mr. Ginsberg saying, "You know, for a big famous guy like Bruce Weber, he was a lot more of a down-to-earth sort of roly-poly happy guy, nice fellow."

Our day with Mr. Ginsberg was far from over. We went from Bruce's place over to Chinatown to 76 Mott Street to eat at Mr. Ginsberg's favorite Chinese restaurant called the Mayflower Tea Parlor. It was a little dive full of Chinese waiters who kept calling him "young man." We talked about his writings and travels with Kerouac and William Burroughs over a dish he had ordered called Gruel (pig intestines) that he insisted we all taste. He talked about his life, it seemed, in a very honest true humble way, often more like a fan of his old friends than as one of their peers.

After about an hour we left the Mayflower Tea Parlor and continued our journey through endless herb-and-root ancient Chinese shops on backstreets down and off Mott and Elizabeth that I don't even think my mother had ever heard of. We were in search of an herb called bitter melon that Mr. Ginsberg took as prescribed by his "guru."

Our journey took us through at least a dozen mystical shops on our endless search for a prescription that I don't think anyone except him and maybe a handful of lifetime Chinatown residents even knew existed. He would pronounce it "bit-ter-melon," and said that it was good for the liver. We never found any bitter melon, but he eventually settled for some other form of root to put in his tea that would supposedly do the same job.

After Chinatown, the rest of the band all went home and Mr. Ginsberg took me over to an art show up on Broadway. It was full of whacked-out modern art. He pointed out a collage of soap on Brillo boxes, explaining the significance of it and that he knew the artist. After a very educated, detailed explanation, he added, "Or of course it could just be a big pile of junk," with his three-second lost pause and then quiet inside laugh.

We left the show and he said he had to get back home to work on an introduction to a book of dreams by Jack Kerouac, a piece he was already five years late on. We said good-bye. I thanked him for the day and promised to find him his bitter melon. When I went home I got a call from a friend of mine who was a big fan of Allen Ginsberg's. He wanted to know what he was like, if he talked a lot about Kerouac and his old stories and writings. I told him we got naked and high, went to Chinatown, ate pig intestines, and searched endlessly for bitter melon. He laughed and wanted to know what we really did.

A few months later Mr. Ginsberg invited me to see him perform his poetry at a place downtown called The Bottom Line. I remember thinking it would probably get pretty boring just hearing someone talk for an hour but I told him I'd go anyway, more out of respect than want. When I got there I noticed he was opening for Ray Manzarek, who had been the keyboard player for The Doors. The audience was real young and obviously there for Ray Manzarek, since The Doors' movie had just come out. When Allen Ginsberg came onstage he looked exactly the same as when I met him. Very plain and ordinary with his glasses in his white short-sleeved sport-shirt pocket. I was afraid the audience would ignore him. He sat down looking as confused and baffled as I had remembered. One stick of incense was burning to his right and a one-note instrument called a harmonium was on his arm as he sat in a small fold-out chair all alone in the middle of this great big stage. He adjusted his microphone for a second as the crowd talked on, paying him no mind. You could kind of hear him, as usual half-saying to himself, "OK, uh, here we go, ah, all right." He then burst into his ranting at top volume with his harmonium, singing and talking away beautiful and funny. He was just like I remembered. Just when you would think he was gone, out of it, he'd be right on. Never in my life have I ever seen anyone captivate an audience the way he did. It was incredible. Through all his singing and yelling and talking and whispering and chanting and anything, there was complete silence. And it was all real. I mean he would talk to the audience just like he was talking to one person, you, or me, alone. He talked of happiness and loneliness, his fear of dying, everything. In one of his stories he talked about eating his egg in the morning and looking out his window to the Mary Help of Christians Church and watching the pigeons and nuns and Avenue A freaks all walking down Loisaida Avenue. "I was there and I looked out that very same window," I remember wanting to tell the guy and girl sitting next to me.

I felt in touch with everything he said. Whether it was about a quiet monastery in China or eating pierogies and kielbasa at the Kiev Diner on 2nd Avenue and 6th Street. He talked about it all with strength and admiration and sadness, and madness, and beauty, and I can never do those same things again without thinking about it like a poet. When he finished, the crowd of about seventy-five people was silent. One by one, after a "Wow!" five-second pause, the whole place began clapping.

After the show, I was standing outside on 5th Avenue when he came up to me and said jokingly, or maybe not, "So you didn't think I could sing, huh?" I told him it was unbelievable and he said, "It's what I do, I've been at it for a while."

The next day I went and got two books of his from the library. I read *Howl* and some other poems. If I had read his writings before, I probably would have gotten bored, but it made sense now.

I went to visit Mr. Ginsberg at his apartment about a year later. He had just come off the road after about three months of touring. He looked beat. What better word to describe a tired Allen Ginsberg than "beat?" I told him I read a lot of his stuff and was now a big fan. He laughed and said, "Oh, *Howl?*" I told him I enjoyed his talking about the Kiev Diner and New York even more. He showed me some pictures he had just taken of William Burroughs naked holding up a rifle in Kansas. They were wild. I played him a song on my guitar. He said he liked it but asked me about certain lyrics. It was pretty cool being able to tell Allen Ginsberg about something I had written. While we were talking he got a phone call. A good friend of his, Harry Smith, had just died. Very straight and formally he thanked the person on the other end for letting him know. He paused for a moment, told me what had happened, and came over to show me a picture he had taken of Harry Smith.

It was a picture of the oldest-looking man I had ever seen pouring milk into a cup. He told me it was one of his favorite pictures. He paused and said, "Tayatha, Gate, Gate Paragate Parasamgate Bodhi Svaha." Surprised, as always, I asked him what that all meant. He said, "Gone Gone Gone Real Gone Peace. Oh you know Dito, Life. It's good to be alive. On with the celebration!"

SAN FRANCISCO

through all of the ups and downs of being in Gutterboy, there's one time that stands out above all others. It was before it all. Before all the record companies and lawyers and managers. When everything was pure and good and fun and music. It was, as Cherry Vanilla would say, "The best time of your life that you'll never realize until another time in your life."

We were playing around town at all the local New York dives—CBGB's, the Lismar Lounge, everywhere. All our friends from the neighborhood would come down to see us, get drunk, and have a real good time. All of a sudden we found ourselves

154

At my kitchen table, Berenice Abbot's vision of Manhattan Xmas eve 1936 above their heads - Gutterboy proud of new Album, named after St. Stanislaus Bishop & Martyr R.C. Church on E. 7th Street between Ave A. & First Ave - September 12, 1991. Allen Ginsberg

(photo: Allen Ginsberg)

128

in just about every New York magazine. Out of nowhere our shows started getting more and more packed. Record companies began coming to see us and we had never even made a demo tape. In a few short months we went from being this local drunken band with an audience full of neighborhood fights to this real hip local drunken band with an audience full of neighborhood fights. Our shows started selling out. It was weird not seeing Tommy Byrnes, Little John, Frankie Rock, Boo Boo, and half the neighborhood out there all alone throwing things at us and each other. Now, along with them were all these mysterious-looking guys in suits taking notes and bringing along these real trendy model-looking girls all dressed in black, getting pushed around by all our own neighborhood girls.

Then one day it happened. Island Records offered us fifty thousand dollars to make an album. I couldn't believe it. I had never even thought about fifty thousand dollars in a realistic way before. We then picked up these two managers from the Upper West Side of Manhattan who told us not to jump on it. They said that if we waited a while we would get better offers. I was going nuts. Fifty thousand dollars seemed like more than enough for me and I didn't want to blow our big chance. Against our managers' wishes I started showing up at record companies just taking any meetings, because even just talking about all that money and big plans was a dream in itself.

To calm us down our managers bought us five round-trip tickets to San Francisco so we could disappear for two weeks. They booked a show at CBGB's for the weekend we would get back and told us that it was the right thing to do. I called up Kat, a friend of mine who had moved to San Francisco. I told her we were coming out and asked if we could all stay at her house for a few days. She said sure and that she would try and help us book some shows when we got there.

Two days later we went to LaGuardia Airport. It was the first time our drummer, Johnny, and I had been on an airplane and our first time out of New York. When we walked on the plane with all of our guitar cases and shaved heads the passengers looked at us like we were either five famous musicians or a gang of armed radical terrorists. I can't tell you how great it all felt. We were on top of the world. Our bass player even ended up fooling around with a beautiful stewardess in the bathroom.

As we flew over America, I remember looking down at the clouds and thinking how wild it all looked. I kept thinking about my ex-girlfriend Lari Anne. She used to tell me about traveling, how much she loved it, how New York wasn't everything. We used to fight like dogs about it because to me, New York had it all.

I could never understand why anyone would want to leave. I'd tell her that if she wanted to go to China, we'd go down to Mott Street in Chinatown. If she wanted Italy we could go down to Mulberry Street. I'd tell her Puerto Rico and Africa were uptown, while Poland and Israel were only a token away downtown. But up in the sky, I could feel everything changing. It was like now that I finally had left, nothing would ever be the same.

We arrived in San Francisco on a Friday afternoon. That night Kat booked us to play at a place called The Stone, opening for a big singer named Chris Isaak. We were picked up at the airport by a local small-time booking agent named Mark Landar, whom Kat had hired to help get us some shows. Mark Landar showed up wearing a straw hat and bright green farmer pants with one bare foot hanging out the window of his five-hundred-year-old Volkswagen Bug that we all somehow managed to pack into with our guitars. For the entire drive we listened to his static-ridden AM radio trying to squeeze out "Cat Scratch Fever" while Mark Landar talked at twice the volume about all the big shows he was working on for us.

Mark Landar's speaking volume—and unexpected moments of painfully loud, obscene outbursts always followed by a great and unbelievable twitch—left us hysterically laughing for the entire drive trying to figure out if he was suffering from Tourette's, deafness, or just complete berserkery.

He drove us straight to the club we were playing at and as we arrived the first thing I saw was our name up in lights. It was a dream. We were three thousand miles away from home and there it was in big giant letters, **GUTTERBOY**. Within twenty minutes of arriving at The Stone, while we were all busy stargazing at our name up in lights, dreaming of fame and fortune and just the whole idea of being in San Francisco, Mark Landar took this as his opportunity, amid a cocaine binge, to rob the first cash register he saw and vanish from everyone he had ever known in San Francisco, including Kat, never to reappear.

About half an hour later the owner of The Stone told us what had happened and canceled our show. But Gutterboy, being well schooled in the bizarre and unexpected, picked up and took our act across the street to a little jazz dive called Teddy's Smoking House. We talked the owner into letting us play there, promising to alter our sound to a more Frank Sinatra, "Strangers in the Night" type of mood. What we didn't let him know was that outside of power chords, distortion boxes, and screaming, we really didn't have very much to offer.

About an hour after we left a message with Kat about what had happened at The Stone, and where we were, she showed up at Teddy's Smoking House with a heavy metal band she managed named Vain. Vain brought down a bunch of their groupie strippers. The strippers brought down a bunch of bikers while our sax player, Barbara, met up with a crew of transvestites from the Castro and brought them along. In no time we had transformed this quiet little half-dead jazz place into a freak show. The last thing I can remember about that night was doing an unbearably unrecognizable, intoxicated version of "New York, New York" while down on all fours doing push-ups for some unknown reason.

I woke up with my legs still on stage and my head about two feet lower, on the floor. When I got up to look around I saw the band was all huddled up sleeping in one corner while Kat and a bunch of her gang were lying all over the place on tables and chairs. The owner of the club was an old man about seventy-five who wore a purple fedora. The fact that he had somehow managed to fall asleep all propped up face first against a wall with Barbara's saxophone led me to believe that he too had joined in our party.

We had now been in San Francisco for a total of about ten hours and as I walked around at 7 A.M. surveying the obviously finished product of over-partying with transvestites, strippers, and bikers, I wasn't too sure of much except that the first Gutterboy tour had definitely begun.

Since our booking agent was now a missing and wanted outlaw, we took it upon ourselves to go out and get our own shows.

A few days later three friends of ours from New York—Ray Parada, Matty O'Brien, and Chris McGerty—came out to stay with we who were nowhere, anywhere, and everywhere.

We spent the next two weeks like a gang of gypsies running all over town trying to get shows and places to sleep. During our fifteen days in San Francisco we played twelve nights in any old dive that would have us. One night we'd be in a jazz house, the next in some heavy-metal club, and then we'd do a lunchtime acoustic set for vegetarians on Haight Street. We were sort of like five musical chameleons attempting anything just so we could play.

We did a show one night in a place called Route 66. I don't even know how we found it, a real redneck rodeo bar in the middle of nowhere that looked like something straight out of "Gunsmoke." The band that was on before us were all wearing giant cowboy hats, and after five or six Lynyrd Skynyrd covers, ended their set with a song called "Rock and Roll Hoochie Koo" that brought the house down. Wild Turkey was being served everywhere and an electric rodeo horse was spinning a crazy cowboy around in the back, while the five of us from New York all with our heads shaved, including Barbara's, took the stage. Understandably, the place suddenly got pretty quiet. We started our first song and to our surprise they loved it. While I was on stage one madman with spurs asked me who our barbers were and handed me a shot of Wild Turkey. Next I knew, we were attempting "Sweet Home Alabama." It was a great night.

We did another show at a place called The Oasis. There was a giant pool in the center of the dance floor and our friend Matty O'Brien jumped into it in pursuit of the mermaids who'd been hired by the club to swim around. After getting thrown out of The Oasis we met up with a wild girl named Lady Trash. Our system for finding places to sleep was that halfway through our set on stage we would ask the audience, "Who's having a party?" Just about every night we'd end up at some freaked-out house or apartment. This time we met Lady Trash.

Trash was a part-time biker and tattoo artist. She was real nice and sweet and invited us to stay at her place in the Mission District for as long as we needed.

When we arrived at her apartment we couldn't believe our eyes. I have never seen more people living in one house. It was a two-story house with twenty dogs, cats, rabbits, and probably just about every last leftover acid casualty from the '60s. Everywhere you could possibly go there were people either hanging out getting high, playing guitars, sleeping, or up to some form of weirdness.

The first night at Trash's I met this really beautiful Spanish stripper who was crashing there and slept in a park with her. Lady Trash helped us out with a few more shows at some biker hangouts and took us around on kind of her own underground tour of San Francisco.

We spent fifteen days in San Francisco running, high, up and down Haight Street chasing girls, playing shows, finding new places to sleep every night and just wandering around being New Yorkers in a foreign land. The whole time we were there we didn't once think about any of the record companies, going home, or even sleeping for that matter. It was the moment, and it was an incredible moment.

Our last night we played at a place called The Works. It was a combination pizzeria–pinball hangout–drag queen nightclub. Everyone showed up. We had a big party and played some new songs. We drank and laughed. It was pouring rain out and we put on a tape of Chet Baker. There was a song on it called "I Get Along Without You Very Well." It was about leaving and in our drunken states we got sad and melancholy for a minute. But when you're young and a song makes you sad, you get up and change it. So we got up, put on *Damaged* by Black Flag and drank and smoked all night long.

While we were flying home the next morning I remember having a feeling I never had before. When I left New York I felt kind of weird but I knew I would be back soon and everything would go back to normal, or at least normal abnormality. But for the first time in my life I felt like I was really leaving somewhere, and it was sad. I had never done that before.

THE MOST
SUCCESSFUL
UNSUCCESSFUL
BAND IN HISTORY

when we got back from San Francisco things got even more crazy. We were the talk of the town. Every record company was after us. We eventually signed to Geffen Records. A *Vanity Fair* article claimed that at one million dollars, our signing was the biggest in history for a new band. Nothing seemed real at the time. We were being driven around in limousines and flying off first-class everywhere.

Geffen booked a small tour for us to play up and down the East Coast. Two vanloads of friends from our neighborhood came along. In our brief two-week tour, I believe we were banned from every single club we played at, from The 930 in

D.C. to The Channel in Boston. The wildest thing I can remember about that tour was being chased out of the state of Rhode Island, throwing rocks and bottles out the open back doors of our speeding van to deter the mob of locals from continuing their chase.

When we returned to New York we were asked to do a show for Geffen Records at a Hawaiian landmark restaurant uptown on 51st Street called The Hawaii Kai. When we arrived on the night of the show there was a midget bouncer at the door named Pee Wee, hula dancers on stage, and a guy playing a ukulele in the back. I looked over to Barbara for a second as she gave me that "so what else is new" shrug.

The last thing I can remember about our show at The Hawaii Kai was lying down on stage, high out of my mind, singing "Bye Bye Miss American Pie" with my girl Lisa Marie, while half the club was being set on fire by my friends, who at the time were being chased out by Pee Wee with a rifle.

The next day I called up Michael Rosenblatt, one of our A&R record people at Geffen, to see if he liked the show. He said he liked the first fifteen minutes of the set but had to leave after a molotov cocktail hit his table and set it on fire. A week later I drew my friend E.J. a map of the Geffen Records offices in Rockefeller Center. He planned to bring his demo tape there and wanted to be sure they would remember him. He painted himself red, put on a clear mask, and ran completely naked through the Geffen offices screaming and throwing his demo tapes everywhere while I held the elevator door open for him, wearing a ski mask. Three security guards were punched and knocked over that day by two extremely identifiable intruders and Gutterboy was looking for a new record label a month later.

That winter we signed to Polygram Records and finally made a record that actually came out in stores. We recorded it with a producer named Charlie Midnight. Charlie was a big brawny Brooklynite who had worked with James Brown. I loved recording with Charlie. He reminded me of the guys I had grown up with. He'd look at you, and with his real Brooklyn accent deliver his best line: "Hey, look at me, I'm living proof mediocrity can succeed, so don't worry."

We asked to make the record in Los Angeles, but ended up stuck in a townhouse that was rented for us by the record company in a suburb of New Jersey. They thought we'd all be safer and could keep out of trouble there.

For the two months that we were recording in the once quiet town of West Orange, New Jersey, two suburban houses right in the center of town were turned into freak headquarters. It was madness. Everybody, everything, and anything from nudity to guns, to drugs, to pre-ops, post-ops, and guidos were now residents of West Orange. There were loud, crazy Puerto Rican drag queens drinking 180-proof on the porch while we were running naked by the pool, with half our neighborhood from Astoria chasing the local college girls around.

After a near Frankenstein-like torch-gathering farewell from the people of West Orange we left town and headed out on the road as the opening act on the Stray Cats reunion tour.

We went through half of America with the Stray Cats, pulling into late-night truck stops in Ames, Iowa, roaming through nowhere places down back roads in South Carolina, playing baseball on our days off with Amish kids in Intercourse, Pennsylvania. We got high with naked girls in Minnesota and stayed up all night in haunted hotels in Chicago. And then zooming through empty 3 A.M. nowhere roads in middle America playing endless *Monopoly, Trivial Pursuit,* and a horrible sort of password game our roadie Matt Melnick had invented called *Name the Disease.*

Matt: Shortness of breath, endless pain, lesions on body.
Band: Um, um, leprosy?

We'd pull up into half-lit neon-blinking late-night lost phonebooths, braving the spiderwebs, putting in our last quarters to tell her how much we missed her and then jump back on board and continue. At sunrise I'd wake up, sit up front with Billy the bus driver and just look out at the most beautiful America I had ever seen. One great day off in Indiana we all went down and played a wild hunting paintball shooting game with a bunch of local Marines. Almost every night we'd share this sort of half sleep because "you-can't-wait-for-the-new-day" to the sounds of our nightly dose of Chet Baker and Art Pepper as Billy would drive us across 4 A.M. state borders.

On the road we were playing seven nights a week. Five of them opening for the Stray Cats, and the other two at any local club in any town we were staying that would let us. As crazy and busy and sleepless as it all was I can't ever remember a more fulfilling time in my life. Everything was happening. It was all happening so fast and now, just the way I like it. No tomorrow or big future plans. It was here.

We returned home after about five months of traveling and playing up and down across the country including one brief stop in London where we actually witnessed a near fist fight between Van Morrison, the singer of Simply Red, and a living stereotype of *The Ugly American*. (A hilarious, obese [much missed] giant drunken circular Texan wearing a giant cowboy hat and spitting out enormous amounts of phlegm through his oversized intoxicated mouth while calling them both a couple of "faggot queer limeys!")

Two weeks after getting home we were told by the record company there was no more money for us to tour or make a video. We immediately did what always came naturally and called up everyone we knew that could help us make a free video. Within two days we had three friends with video cameras, two vans with lights that Johnny's uncle had access to, a photographer friend of ours, Lance Staedler, to film it, and unlimited free editing time on weekends at my old friend Big Orlando's job. We called up just about every neighborhood guy that we knew and shot our video in the back alleys of 21st Avenue the next day with a zero-dollar budget. It came out great and premiered on a pay-type of TV jukebox on channel 54 that could be seen all over New York for three dollars a play. The fact that just about everyone in Astoria was in the video, and called in for it, made it the most requested video on that channel for the two months it was on, beating out Michael Jackson and Madonna.

Everywhere we went people were beginning to recognize us. We were being stopped for autographs and were in just about every single magazine you could think of. It had gotten so crazy we were even forced to turn down certain interviews, and when a major band now came to New York, it was us they wanted as their opening act.

On the week that the rest of the country was supposed to share in this phenomenal thing that was happening to us in New York, things started changing. All of a sudden our video was not going to premiere on MTV because of some strange occurrence. The next week our video was taken off the jukebox channel while it was still the most-requested video, with no reason given.

I got a phone call that Friday from our managers telling us that the record company had thought we were a little too wild, out of control, the record wasn't selling, and that they had decided to drop us. I couldn't believe it. I honestly didn't see it coming and had no idea how to break the news to the other guys in the band without it sounding like one of my many jokes.

I sat down staring kind of blankly out my window and listening over and over again to our record. As I listened, all the great thoughts of making it and touring and hearing ourselves for the first time came to me as if they were being projected right there in front of me on the wall. After about an hour with that tenth wind of faith and confidence that somehow always returns in time of need, I stood up, washed my face, greased back my hair, and got ready for the next big fight, knowing we were too good to give up.

The phone rang and it was Barbara. She had heard the news and was calling to say she loved all of us but had finally just got a decent paying job. She felt she had been through too much and didn't think she wanted to continue. I told her, with my own questionable confidence, how we had always made it through the tough times and that we'd pull through this one as well. She said that as hard as it was she had made up her mind and felt it was the right thing to do.

Me and Johnny met up with Eric and Danny at their apartment on 17th Street later that day. We talked about the last four years of our lives together for almost the entire night before deciding to call it quits. Of course Johnny, like me, was all for keeping it going. I mean, if the two of us had our way we'd end up putting out more unwanted records than Engelbert Humperdinck, Tom Jones, and Neil Sedaka combined.

After our night of reminiscing, I put on my coat and got ready to leave. We all said good-bye and headed our separate ways. As I walked through Danny and Eric's long narrow hallway and down their two flights of stairs I thought about the first day after we had gotten signed. I thought about the time we got naked with Allen Ginsberg and about scaring Barbara in our haunted hotel in Chicago. I thought about us running out to buy the first magazine we were ever all in and that completely drunken trip to Miami with Bruce Weber. I thought of our long crazy stay in Woodstock, New York, in the middle of winter, recording our first record with Jonathan Elias and Rod O'Brian, who had just come from recording their other "also famous" groups like Duran Duran and Aerosmith. I thought as far back as Bob Semen and our first managers at High Noon who really believed in us. I thought of all those late-night talks in the back of the bus about how great it all felt, and an interview Barbara had once given saying, when asked what it was like to be the only girl in Gutterboy, that she felt like she was always surrounded by four big brothers. I thought about how we always helped each other out through our tough relationships back home while on the road. I thought about sitting out on that farm in Champagne, Illinois, and playing cool jazz chords with the rest of the guys while Barb blew her sax just right on our day off that week. I remembered, vividly, getting kicked offstage in Delaware for coming out in that college mascot's purple gorilla outfit I found in the dressing room while high out of my mind on Nyquil, since my managers had cut me off from liquor for the duration of the tour. Immediately following that I remember hitting a moment of Nyquil enlightenment outside on the curb while yelling very serious and boldly (and still in gorilla suit from the waist down), "YES MIKE, YES MICHAEL O'SHEA MY VERY GOOD FRIEND, WHEREVER YOU ARE. YOU WERE RIGHT, A MAN IS MEANT TO RUN BARE-CHESTED THROUGH THE FIELDS," before quite anticlimactically fainting on the side of the road in vomit. I thought about all of us showering together in San Francisco and our baseball game against Kool and The Gang in New Jersey. I thought about our dwarfed rehearsal studio owner threatening to kill us for allegedly training bugs to attack him upon command, and that all-expenses-paid trip we took with our friend Matt Green's band to Baltimore when we ended up spending all of our money renting a speedboat that I somehow managed to crash through the front door of the house of the guy who rented it to us. I thought of one beautiful magic night in Texas with Neil Young and Willie Nelson. I remembered the perfect feeling of waking up in a ratty old van on some nowhere tour and not even knowing what state I was in.

I thought about all the times I secretly looked over at Barbara playing her saxophone and fantasized about her being my cool cool jazz wife and us being the hippest couple on

167

167

a guide to recognizing your saint

earth. I thought a million thoughts. A million beautiful thoughts. And I felt that kind of heavy sadness that we all for some real dark reason like to feel. It was that kind of melancholy heavy sadness that you know will soon go away and almost don't even really want to.

As I stepped outside and began heading for my subway home, Eric, the quietest of all of us, called me from his window and said kind of half-energetic half-faint, "Hey, it was cool right?!" with a kind of sincere gravelly tone. I asked him what was cool? He said "Us . . . right?" I said yeah. He kind of nodded, looked up and said, "The coolest."

Interview with DJ Toxic Tommy at WSOU two weeks before band break-up:

> **Toxic Tommy:** So how would you guys define Gutterboy?
>
> **Barbara:** We're the most successful unsuccessful band in history.
>
> **Toxic Tommy:** (laughing) The most successfully unsuccessful band in history?
>
> **Johnny:** No, the most successful unsuccessful band in history.

"I don't want to be famous!" A comedian in Washington Square Park said. "When you get famous they put giant posters of you up in all the subway stations so people can draw dicks on your face . . . I don't want to be famous!"

Authorized advertisement for Calvin Klein underwear

Unauthorized advertisement for gay club in Chicago

photo: Juliet Lofaro

at the video

photo: Lance Staedler

For *Splash* magazine

guide to recognizing your saint

Gutterboy observing Dianne Brill

a guide to recognizing your saint

photo: Lance Staedler

guide to recognizing your saints

phil Ochs stood here

photo: Lance Staedler

a guide to recognizing your saint

IN fashion

MEN & WOMEN

200+
FASHION
BUYS
UNDER
$99

INSIDE:
'70S STYLE:
ROCKS IN
THE '90S

15 HOT NEW
BANDS YOU
SHOULD HEAR

HOW TO THROW
A CHEAP PARTY

FLIRTING WITH
DITO &
SUPERMODEL
EMMA S.

SPRING /SUMMER '9?
U.S. $2.95 / CANADA $3.50

32

0 71486 02886 4

174

healing

guide to recognizing your saint

A CONVERSATION ABOUT DEEPAK CHOPRA WHILE EATING POT COOKIES IN A 2ND AVENUE APARTMENT (THE EGGPLANT WITHOUT HAIR)

so i'm sitting here miles above the earth in some airplane most likely getting closer to California and I'm thinking about something Ray said to me the other day in New York. It was New Year's Eve and we were both crazy high at a party a friend of ours, John Vaccaro, has every year. John is about sixty, everyone there is pretty close to his age and they're all interesting Warhol-like characters sitting around frying to these intensely delicious gourmet meals that he makes marinated in magic mushrooms with delicious and sweet pot cookies as the dessert. While kind of real dreamed-out I told

Ray about a note that a friend of ours who is very sick and near death wrote me, saying, "I love you and we will know each other forever."

I was sad to hear Ray (who is my oldest and closest friend) tell me that he did not believe that after death the spirit remembers this life. In our now almost, wait let me correct that, definite hallucinating state I inquisitively asked, "So you don't believe that after this life there will be any bond to it? You don't think your greatest love, the one you will long for the rest of this life (remember at this point I'd eaten at least a dozen mushrooms), or your absolute most precious friend whom you've poured your deepest of emotions into will even exist in spirit after death?" "Absolutely not!" he answered. "How can that be so?" I said, puzzled as my eyes focused intensely on the lock of an insignificant door for about five minutes until I finally read the inscription on it (MEDCO) and realized I had been staring, in a mushroom glaze, at a door lock for the past five minutes. Ray, who was probably focusing on his own equally interesting fixture in the apartment, then picked the conversation right back up as if there had never been a pause by saying, thickly, liquidly, and slow, "Deepak Chopra." I responded equally as fluidly, "Whaaat?" "Deepak Chopra" he answered. "He is a very enlightened and intelligent man on this level of thought. He says that our bodies here on this earth are like transistor radios." Now check this out because at the time it flipped me out and made all the sense in the world.

He said, "Listen, Dito" (and I did), "Deepak Chopra is a doctor who says that if you were to turn a radio on to a station that is playing Beethoven, Beethoven would be coming out of that radio, but if you were to dissect, break apart, and search every last possible crevice of that radio you would not find Beethoven inside of it. And if you were to then take that same radio with you to Istanbul or even the moon, Beethoven could still be coming out of it, but inside you would still not find Beethoven. Therefore the transistor radio is just a mere vehicle relaying messages, which in this case was the message of Beethoven." Feverishly Ray continued as I very attentively stood there. "The comparison being, that if I were to tear your body completely open" (I winced at the thought), "I would not find Dito inside. Or if you were to cut your finger, a little bit of Dito would not leak out. Therefore, like the transistor radio, your body is just a vehicle parlaying the message of you."

Intrigued, consumed, and overwhelmed, I asked, "Yes Ray, but isn't that a really good argument for the spirit living on beyond this human life?" His reply in a low chuckle kind of hissy rumbling laugh was, "You know, in all reality I don't know what the hell we're even talking about here, but that Hindu chick over there asked me to give her a back rub about an hour ago," while pointing at a very pretty Indian girl, as he literally ran over to her.

I don't know if there is, isn't, or if there really can be any point to this story, but the next day, after coming down from that very strange sort of slow-motion-type high, I asked Ray if he felt that when you get that high on mushrooms or acid or any hallucinogen, if you really are on a different, more intense level of knowledge.

He answered with a very brief story about how he had once asked that very same question to another friend of his who, like Ray, is a joke writer. The guy told him that if Ray did feel like he was thinking up these really hilarious jokes while he was high, that he should write them down and read them the next day and see if they were still funny. The next time he was in that state he laughed hysterically, for an entire night, at just one joke, undeniably the funniest thing he had ever come up with. He got a pen and wrote it down. The following morning, all hungover and sick, he went through his pocket. On a piece of toilet paper, barely legible, crooked, and all crumpled up was written:

The Eggplant without Hair

lori was this real strange sexy-looking
Sephardic Jewish girl, whose Italian father, at the time I was dating her, was being placed by the federal government along with
the rest of her immediate family, into the witness protection
program for being the first mobster to testify against John Gotti
in a court of law.

Lori was also cheating on me. So what I did, which most
people in absurd relationships can probably relate to, was simply try every single numerical combination on Earth to decode
her answering machine and find out what was going on.

During the recording of my first album, between singing, harassing Larry King on AM radio, and pranking just about every late-night Greek coffee shop owner in downtown New York City (Cozy Soup n' Burg), I finally broke it: "2, 5." What had me baffled for so long was that you had to hold the number 2 down for at least a good three seconds before hitting the 5. But halfway through that record I cracked the code on her answering machine and this is what I heard:

Machine: Hello, you have four messages.
1) "beep" (me): "Hello, Lori, it's Dito. Call me back at the studio."
2) "beep" (me): "Lori, where are you? Call me."
3) "beep" (Roseanne "The Hedge"—Lori's nightmare dust-head friend from Howard Beach, Queens, with hair so freaking high it looked like a lawn, hence the name, "The Hedge") "Law (pronounced with much too much cherry-flavored Hubba Bubba in mouth) Law, look, it's not the asshole, pick up the phone."

   (click . . . the sound of the phone being answered)

4) "beep" The Hedge: "Law, pick up (pause), Law (pause), look, it's not Dito, and he's not making me say this (pause) OK, I'll prove it, look (yells) **DITO'S AN ASSHOLE, DITO'S AN ASSHOLE!** (pause) All right, I guess you and Stanley must be getting busy. Have fun."

   (click—hang up)

Be me for a minute, OK? Pick up your phone, call Nerf in Astoria, and tell him to get the hell over to the recording studio as fast as possible with his car. We gonna take a fever ride about one hundred miles an hour up to 91st Street and 2nd Avenue to find out who this Stanley is!

When we got there I was out of my mind. I started climbing up six stories of fire escape to get to her window. When I was four stories high, Nerf yelled up to me with a crazy-looking smile, "Yo Dito, check out what just came on the radio!" as he blasted "Hey Joe" by Jimi Hendrix. Now if this scene were ever in a movie I'd walk out. I wouldn't believe it. It would be too corny. But it really happened, and it was perfect. I mean what a moment. To this day Nerf still brags about the immaculacy of that moment. The way "Hey Joe" came on at that moment was perfect.

Years later, I had another perfect moment. I had been away for a while and arrived in Astoria on a Saturday afternoon in the middle of a heat wave, just as all the guys in the neighborhood were starting up a strike box game on my block. Just like Phil Rizzutto (the Yankee scooter), Kenny Coyle yelled "Play ball" as he hit the play button on a boom box and Frank Sinatra's "Summer Wind" started up. And I knew I was home.

In Washington Square Park on a fall Sunday three crazy black guys with real gone, out-there afros danced the dance to end all dances to the lunacy of that freaked-out kind of electric keyboard '70s guitar solo in the Isley Brothers' "Who's That Lady?" and brought on that feeling once again.

Just like the Greeks did at the Pancyprian Social Club the time we danced "OPA! OPA!" Slapping the heels of our shoes over broken plates: "Aseskunaki! Aseskunaki!"

It happened the day sad Lisa walked out of my room in Astoria for the last time on leaving for Hollywood. I induced it even further by putting on Nina Simone's "I Loves You Porgy" over and over again. Especially that opening line when she says, "Don't let 'em take me."

It happened with the noisy butterflies of Ojo Caliente!

It happened on the happiest craziest night with Ray and Mike after buying ecstasy and other mind-altering fun things from a mad street pharmacist at the Chelsea Hotel and losing all control at Rick's Lounge on 8th Avenue under a multicolored spinning disco ball.

It happened at fifteen, the first time I wandered into the Mudd Club on White Street and saw girls with shaved heads, crazy colored mohawks, loud fastest music on, and thought yes, this is what I've been looking for . . . !

And just like that it happened every time the Bad Brains played "How Low Can a Punk Get" in a packed CBGB's one-hundred-degree pipes sweating chaos . . .

It happened on the way to a fight once while walking all cool and Spanish as someone playing stickball fouled off a Spaulding ball that landed perfectly in my hand, not breaking my stride or motion, in front of a whole stoop full of beautiful Puerto Rican girls, and I knew I looked good . . .

It was my father's tear, first time ever, followed by a strong cover-up hug and "now get out of here" on my leaving New York that brought it that time . . .

It was brought on by her face, under that lamppost, in that rain, before complete night, 7 P.M. Thursday 31st Street corner, and the RR train was going by . . .

. . . and again in Yogaville, Virginia, on Yogi Satchidananda's purple lotus-shaped farm. Go find it, near Norfolk and Farmville. Light of Truth Universal Shrine . . .

. . . and again while dancing drunk and berserk to "Brick House" in the Peppermint Lounge on Tommy Byrnes's shoulders at Kim Smith's birthday party . . .

At thirteen it happened as me and Graziano held our breath in pin-drop silence while hiding under a parked van from a lunatic Greek with a gun and out of nowhere we got this crazy smile on our faces . . .

Behind Our Lady of Mount Carmel Church when me and Ray took a quaalude each and smoked our first *tres* bag of Christmas Tree pot together and somehow had the exact same hallucinations even though we later found out that what we had bought on the corner and smoked were three joints of oregano from Lisa's Pizzeria, and chased them down with two very tasty well-disguised orange St. Joseph's Aspirin . . .

At fifteen, in Gloria and her boyfriend (from the band Bad Posture) seven-foot-three "Fourway's" apartment on Avenue B and 6th Street it happened as I watched Willy "No Edge" shoot up fifteen people with about twenty bags of dope and then go back around with his infamous eyedropper filled with liquid acid as they all laid back in scattered armchairs taking a kind of junkie communion in their eyes, and I thought . . . wow . . . !

And when I took three blows, two to the head and one across my face by a Puerto Rican with a baseball bat on Steinway Street and felt like a man for some crazy reason, it happened again . . . identical to the time Antonio pulled out a pointy-nosed cane from my stomach and said, "Damn, fuckin' Dito, that gotta hurt." And it did . . .

It happened with no one around while waiting for a train on the Prince Street station at 4 A.M. the night Jenny left me drunk in a bar on Mulberry for flirting with some girl . . .

It lasted for four and a half minutes on stage at the Bottom Line club while singing a song called "Growing Up Under the RR" when Cliffy yelled out, "Do this one for one of our boys who went down tonight." On finding out Giuseppi had that day been killed . . . and reminded me immediately of the time I looked through Little Peter Taci's bullet holes in his chin as he lay out in the P.S. 85 school yard near death, and then dead . . .

It happened when I shook Martha Graham's frail hand and she called me handsome . . .

Just as it can be brought on almost any time by shopping at Vaccarro's green bakery for some most delicious giant loaf of bread, then on to Joe's deli on Sullivan Street for a quarter-pound of smoked mozzarella, sun-dried tomatoes, and lots of it. Sneak then on to Vinny Vella's roof with a love, and it will happen.

And of course it happened on that N train. While rushing to Taci Letterman's house during the Mets' ninth inning World Series, as the conductor of the train gave us play-by-play over the loudspeaker and we all decided to just hear the rest of the game there on that train . . . and the Mets won. "Mookie is the man!"

And upon a mixture of overwhelming emotions and reunions. Upon returning after such a long time to very sick father, near-death Angelo, rehabilitated Jimmy, Tommy Byrnes, now proud father of two, and lost-again Cherry. Upon hearing of Antonio's deportation. Upon hearing of so much death and life and sadness and joy. Upon realizing it is no longer home, and saying good-bye for a long time to New York and childhood friends with a closeness only a childhood friend can have. It happened this time like ten thousand thunderous sad quiet beautiful hurricanes. In an airport, LaGuardia, in absolute silence as Mike O'Shea, Ray Parada, Frankie Rock, Jimmy Mullen, and Nerf waved good-bye instead of see ya later.

And with deep breath as it cleansed my soul, brought on that lightening but uplifting heavy light razor sadness, and made it OK to start new life knowing I will possess the old one in heart forever, the song of quiet this time momentarily touched a peace.

And until now, and I mean today, while writing this, the connection between these twenty-six moments was never too clear. But in writing them, reliving all of them here on Vermont Avenue by pen, on paper, I feel twenty-six lives. Twenty-six moments I have truly been alive. Twenty-six moments I knew just where I was. Twenty-six times I felt that clench in my teeth, that flow of life in the back of my jaw, that sensation that goes right up your spine, waters your eyes, and ends up somewhere right behind your ears.

And I understand now, maybe not completely, but more, that in times of overwhelming joy, immobile sadness, hysterical laughter, absolute fear, and sometimes just perfect quiet there is Life. Real Life. And it really is that simple. I take my gift now. I go live.

Oh and by the way, about Lori. You remember, the girl I was going up the fire escape after when "Hey Joe" came on. The one who started me off in this direction for a chapter. What did finally happen when I got to her living-room window on the sixth floor that night was, unfortunately, not as romantic as all the visions it induced, though probably as passionate. She was walking out of her bedroom naked and smoking a cigarette (bad sign).

When I tapped on her window to get her attention she screamed like hell had come to her house (hell *had* come to her house!). While screaming she ran into her bedroom which was out of view from my perch. From there I heard a male voice (Stanley) yell, "What the hell is going on?" I jumped through the window. I don't mean kicked in and then went through. I mean, literally crashed through her window, falling over the television. I kicked in her bedroom door and beat the hell out of some naked guy whom up until that point you could say had gotten "lucky" on this very unlucky night.

After Lori scratched, bit, and pulled a handful of crewcut hair out of my head, told me to get the FUCK OUT! and then turned down my marriage proposal (something all guys for some strange reason do in these sort of situations), I left.

On my way down the stairs the cops were already on their way up. I hid my bloodied hands and said to them, quite bothered, "They're freakin' crazy up there, always fighting." The cops ran up right past me. I ran down, got into Nerf's car to some quite unmonumental song on the radio, and went back to the studio. Night done, relationship over, moment captured.

187

THE FIRST
COLD BREEZE
OF SEPTEMBER

The first cold breeze of September came through here today. I got scared and sad, depressed, bummed out, summer's gone, spring's far away, fire hydrants closed, Astoria pool will fill with snow, freezing winter's coming again. Everybody loves New York's fall but me! The trees get pretty, but WINTER'S COMING! I imagined waiting up on Queensborough Plaza for my N train home in that cold, and then I stopped.

I thought . . . wait a minute.
what am I thinking here.

I'm three thousand miles away!
It doesn't get cold here
Pools don't close
Queensborough Plaza doesn't even exist here.

And I got bummed out all over again.

IS IT POSSIBLE
TO GET CLOSER
TO GOD IN A PEEP
SHOW BOOTH

hey god, can I be honest with you? Can I tell you how I truly feel about something I know I'm not supposed to talk to you about? God, when I come with a girl, sometimes I look at her and she's beautiful. I mean like an angel, and I never want to leave. Other times I just want to get the hell out of there. But I seldom, if ever, think of you. When I take the N train down to 42nd and Broadway late at night though, get out and walk between 7th and 8th Avenue, looking at all the neon lights, Peepland (the big eye on 42nd), the scattered hookers, pimps, transvestites, and wandering lost crazies, oh, and when I go into usually Show World on 42nd and 8th and get a handful of tokens to the sounds of some crazy old '70s "Fly Robin Fly" type of song blaring through those crazy Corvette lifetime-warranty speakers, only to be interrupted by some static-ridden insane "barker" telling me there are "openings upstairs for pussy inspectors," and that the girls on the third floor are not only naked, but beautiful. Man, and when I go into one of those luxury seated booths watching some beautiful live Cuban sex happening on a rotating wood paneled platform. Or one with a channel select button, especially years ago when each booth had a photo and a perfect description written by the clean-up guy, on what was going on in it. Yeah that's when I think of you. That's when I think of Heaven. When I remember standing outside Orange Julius or Nedick's in the freezing-cold zero-degrees Christmas Eves, selling those old stale cashews ($1.25 a quarter pound), staring at posters of Seka and Vanessa Del Rio! That's when I think of how hard we would try just to sneak in here. I can sometimes even hear the old sounds of fifteen-year-old naive Giuseppi's and Graziano's laughing and yelling from the next booth what channel to change to. "Yo Dito, there's a guy fucking a pig in this one!!"

You see I know this all probably sounds crazy, but when I'm here God, I think of prayer and sin and dying and getting to Heaven. I wonder if what I'm doing right now is a sin, and I feel lost. Sometimes real lost. I think of how bad I want to find you and get closer to you.

And all the sadness, worrying, and all that confusion seems to go away when I'm here. I know it's all just temporary, it always is. I don't even think it's the high. Like heroin and love, most of the fun is in finding it.

And God, I know you can feel what I feel because I feel it all through you.

And I know you can hear me because I've talked to you from
   here many times before.
And why is it to this day that I still say her name every time
   I come.

EXPLAINING
MAYBERRY

Mayberry is in the heart.

Mayberry is content.

Mayberry is quiet and peace. Inner peace.

Mayberry is strike box up 24th Avenue with fifteen old friends.

Mayberry is a quiet Monday night at a seven o'clock dark down on Prince and Sullivan streets, laughing with Mike O'Shea.

Mayberry is eating dinner over at Graziano's six brothers' and three sisters' noisiest Italian house down Astoria Boulevard.

Mayberry is holding your love by the fountain on a late
        night at 52nd and 6th when everything quiets
        down, and everyone goes home from their long
        trouble-filled days at work.
It's holding the one you love and not thinking of another
        far away.

Mayberry is ignorance of all the want of our great giant New
York City, and the content of your small neighborhood.

Van Morrison says you gotta get a job, a home, a wife. It's
there, you'll find it.

Dylan Thomas drank himself to death at the White Horse
Tavern on Hudson Street looking for it while Tony Delasandro
found it in Betty Deluca, two kids, and a nine-to-five, unloading
trucks right over there, across the street from Hoyt Park.

FURTHER
EXPLAINING
MAYBERRY

when i was a kid i used to always watch *The
Andy Griffith Show*. It took place in a town called Mayberry,
which for some reason seemed like a kind of heaven to me. I
always assumed it was in Indiana. It just seemed like Indiana was
the kind of place somewhere like Mayberry would be.

One particular episode of *The Andy Griffith Show* always
stuck in my head. To be honest I don't even remember what it
was about. It was really just this one scene. Andy Griffith was
sitting out on his porch with his girlfriend, Opie, and Don
Knotts. He was playing the guitar. It was dark and warm and
from that day on I always wanted to be there. Look, I know

how corny this all sounds but for some reason that just seemed perfect to me.

Lately I've been real down and out. I mean I feel real lost and confused and I don't really know what to do. I just came off the road after three long months of touring with my band in just about every dive across the country. I'm tired but I don't want to sleep. I took a walk around the neighborhood and no one's around. Sometimes I wonder if it's all worth it. I'm thinking of what Van Morrison says. I'm thinking of Tir Na Nog, eternal youth, happiness, all that crazy shit. Content of the heart. Content from within. Just melancholy quiet with a love at my side.

It's just all this want and chase and longing, when all I truly long for is to be content. Mayberry with ten old friends, a home, a job, and a love.

I finally made it to Indiana for the first time on this tour. I was in Detroit with my band and we got a last-minute call telling us one more date had been added to our tour in Indiana. I got real excited. Finally, Mayberry. On the road that night, at one of our endless late-night all-night truck stops off route anywhere, I picked up a map of Indiana in search of my Mayberry, without much luck.

The next morning we pulled into Indianapolis, Indiana. I remember getting out of the bus and looking at this great giant fountain. I was thinking that it did kind of look a bit like Mayberry, but without any dirt roads. To be honest it looked a lot more like Willoughby, which is sort of another form of Mayberry except that Willoughby is an imaginary town from *The Twilight Zone*. That's a whole other story though and I'm sure this all seems pretty whacked out enough as it is.

That night when we went on stage to play I was a bit drunk. I asked the audience with a sort of intoxicated mumble just where the hell Mayberry was? I told them my dreams about

Mayberry as a child and that I was sure I was in the right state but just didn't know where to look. Everyone laughed. I guess they didn't realize how serious I was.

After the show the other three guys in the band, as usual, would leave with all the pretty girls. Barbara, our sax player, as always would go back on the bus and get high with all the local subterraneans. While I, for some reason, always attracted the local overweight drunken guy with a shirt that would read something like, "50 Reasons Why a Beer Is Better than a Woman."

This night, being like any other on the road, he was there. This time he came in the form of a giant sort of John Madden football type. He had a hat on with a pair of horns coming out of each side. And like clockwork, just as I was attempting to head over toward all the pretty girls, I heard with a real nasty drunken hard-to-understand loud slurred voice, "You kicked fuckin' ass up there, let me buy you a beer." So as everyone else went on partying through the night, I retired over to the bar with Randy Ruckter, local tractor-trailer driver, consumer of beer, and American traveler whose hobbies included arm wrestling, fighting in general, and popping beer caps open with his eyelids (he demonstrated).

As me and Randy sat drinking away in this middle-of-nowhere club somewhere in Indiana, he mumbled something about, "If you want Mayberry, it's in North Carolina." I asked him where and he said it was filmed in a town called Raleigh and that Aunt Bee from the show was now completely insane and still lived there with a million cats. I thanked Randy Ruckter for the information and in absolute drunken confidence told him my dreams and longings for Mayberry.

I haven't yet made it to Raleigh, North Carolina. I'm pretty sure the show was filmed there, though. I can't tell you how many times I've heard that same old cat story about Aunt Bee since then.

One day I hope to make it to Raleigh, but for me Mayberry will always be in Indiana. Mayberry will always be in the heart. In the soul. So go on now. You go find your Mayberry, and if you find the real one, let me know.

Eddie calls my family a "bus stop waiting to happen."

THE MONDAY
NIGHT PACE

I was thousands and thousands of
miles away from all of my old ghosts. It was late and I was
watching a videotape of the movie *Desperately Seeking Susan*
and it brought me back.

I was paying no attention to it, but for a good fifteen to
twenty minutes I just sat there staring at the television with
that kind of glazed 3-D glare watching you, me, Ray, and
Mike and all of those old ghosts just walking around freezing downtown. It wasn't anything too dramatic. To be honest, in the vision we looked kind of bored and cold. I

mean, we were half smiling and all, but for the most part we were just walking along keeping up that sort of quiet Monday night pace. And nothing could have been more perfect than that.

YOU THINK
YOU'VE SEEN
THE BEST MINDS
OF YOUR
GENERATION
WASTED

and when willie deville's wandering

junked-out always hip soul roams aimlessly up and down
Christopher Street with his not-too-famous but signature white
undershirt, painted-on skinny mustache, long Spanish 1950s
sideburns and that little rabid-looking pound-awaiting ASPCA
calendar poodle, do you think he is then hearing the choir sing
"Ave Maria?" Is he then still having that same recurring dream?
Man, he wrote that song. It was called "Heart and Soul" and it
should have been a hit.

And do you think Leonard knows that if it weren't for that
line about Suzanne taking him down to the river and feeding

him that wild combination of tea and oranges that came all the way from China, well does he know if it weren't for that, he too could be marching down that very same, already much too crowded, B side of the street?

And then there's Jake La Motta (The Raging Bull), the comedian Lenny Bruce, the baseball player Shoeless Joe, the trumpet player Chet Baker, along with at least a dozen other, almost forgotten legends if it weren't for the grace of a few reminiscing movie producers.

But why are we mourning here for these people? They've all had their fifteen minutes of fame! They've felt the electricity of shouting fans! They have at least touched the breath of notoriety! What of all the Triple A ball players that never get picked? Even deeper than that, what of all the faceless potential Joe DiMaggios who will never even make it out of their own neighborhood school yards? Or the future Bob Dylans or Phil Ochses who will sing their songs forever down long acoustic subway tunnels to the mad rush of midtown nine-to-fivers paying no mind to them at all?!

Bukowski's brilliance got real lucky one day and ended up on the tables of a thousand college kids who all share that same fantasy of becoming drunken alcoholic miserable homeless heartbroken poets. Well, do you think that same thing happens even one-tenth of one-tenth of a percent of the time? Man, everybody knows there's only one Jack Kerouac for every ten thousand Dean Moriartys. One storyteller to every fifty stories, one picture for a lifetime of memories. Jerry Nolan summed it all up in an article he wrote for the *Village Voice* about the passing of his friend and fellow New York Doll, Johnny Thunders, by simply saying, "It sucks, but sometimes you just get screwed." And two weeks later, just as everyone in town was talking about how he should go on and write a book about all of those great adventures with the Dolls, he dropped dead in some ratty East Village dive.

Justice is not always served. I did, however, hear that Frankie Lymon's old band, The Teenagers, just won some big lawsuit, finally giving them back millions of dollars and the copyrights to a few of their great hits like "Why Do Fools Fall in Love?"

So how do you finally define or explain the whole balancing of these scales of fate? How do we explain the reasoning behind why The Teenagers finally got what they deserved, when you just know there's a kid in some nowhere cornfield in Ames, Iowa, hitting 500-foot home runs to the applause of no more than six or seven friends and family members?

The best way I can explain it came not so long ago to me. It happened with my band. Things had been going great for us. For the entire previous year we were in magazines, tour buses, and limousines. All of a sudden it was all gone. Everything was taken away and there was nothing we could do to change it. We all disappeared from each other for a while. None of us even spoke about it to anyone.

We got a call about a month later saying that we had three days of free studio time to record some new songs. We were all kind of wary about going in, but after seeing each other for no less than fifteen minutes we were sure we wanted to do it. The next three days were spent in absolute bliss. It was like nothing had ever happened. We were all up to the same old craziness, joking with each other, fooling around. And although in the backs of our minds we knew we were only on a sort of three-day pass from all of our recent misfortunes, it really didn't matter because we were doing what we loved. We weren't in there trying to write the next big hit. We were in there because it was what we did. And it was then that the answer to this great mystery came to me, the answer being that the reason we all really do the things that we do isn't because of all the outside rewards, it's because of the inside ones. And the only difference between the recognized ones and the unrecognized ones can best be defined by my friend Frankie when he says, "It's like being somewhere great and not having a picture to show for it. But you were still there and sometimes maybe that's better."

And no less than a minute later, like some haunting echo, I could feel the presence of Johnny Friendly summoning every has-been, could-have-been, should-have-been, would-have-been, is them, all of them, all of us.

I could have had class,
I could have been a contender,
I could have been somebody instead of a bum, which is what I am.
Let's face it. It was you Charlie,
It was you.

And as his voice rang through every late-night subway station, ratty old boxing gym, backfield baseball diamond, and neighborhood bar, tonight it was OK. For tonight, and only for tonight, the answer to this forever mystery was in our possession. Tonight on 57th Street, Bill Cunningham, the paparazzo of paparazzis, will be photographing all of those brilliant minds you spoke of in that poem about all of those writers and musicians and artists all running mad and aimlessly down Avenue D for a fix just to forget what it was (is) they are all so capable of doing. And tonight, as our glorious Pied Piper of fallen dreams would say . . .

I will think of Dean Moriarty
I will think of Dean Moriarty
I will think of Dean Moriarty

photo: Lance Staedler

photo: Juliet Lofaro

a guide to recognizing your saint

Acting tough, indifferent, sexy, self-absorbed, forward looking & relaxed together so they don't even have to pay attention to each other, Gutterboy on the roof under Empire State Building's diplomat spire, ▓▓▓▓ September 13, 1991. Allen Ginsberg

ANONYMOUS

i heard about a geisha from Gion, Japan. Her life was beautiful, sad, unbelievable. She understood the value in such a life. In her old age, while one day crossing Park Avenue in New York City, she was struck with a thought. All that the people passing in their mad rushes in this city noticed, if they noticed anything at all, was a little old Japanese woman standing on the corner in a kimono. "Do they know where my life has taken me!"

This story brought many people to mind. Jimmy Mullen, more than anyone. The most beautiful and talented songwriter

I have ever known. One of the most beautiful people I've ever known. Do you know who he is?

He stands on the corner of St. Mark's these days a lot. Just another ex-junkie on methadone fading into that Avenue D backdrop. What a bore. I know who he is, though. He doesn't fade in. Ever. None of you do. I'm a lucky guy!

HEALING

i'm on my way over to a bar on Lexington
Avenue and 26th Street called Tom O'Reilly's to see my friend
Mike O'Shea's band play. I'm coming from sparring at the Julio
Rivera boxing gym on E. 11th Street. It's late and it's a Saturday
night. The streets are full of crazies and lovers and gangs of
laughing people. But tonight all I can think about is Annette.

Whenever she was in town we would go right over there to
that sixty-cent frankfurter and papaya stand and get the $2.10
special, two frankfurters and a papaya juice. (Hell, maybe that's
the reason why she ain't around.) When we first met I fell in
love with her in half a minute. You must remember. She had the

most beautiful eyes and smile and voice I had ever seen or heard. I just loved being around her. We'd roam up and down the city until all hours of the night just talking, fooling around, making love in crazy places.

She won't call now for some reason and it's driving me crazy. But it's always like that. I don't only mean with her. It's like that with everything. I remember thinking Lari Anne was my love forever and after her it was Lori and then Lisa.

I'm real sad about Annette. I'm running from phone to phone trying to reach her. I've got that image of Woody Allen on 7th Avenue in my head again and it's driving me nuts. I feel like I really messed up, but that's why I wrote all of this craziness anyway. I wrote it because life goes on. I wrote it because people change and people leave, and new things come along. I wrote it because when Tony Bennett sings, or the Philharmonic plays under a beautifully moonlit Central Park sky, or some unknown saint disguised as your everyday passerby stops to say a kind word in a time of need, you know someone's out there.

I realize now that the reason we often feel so bad about change is because of all those beautiful things that happen in our lives. I mean, I can't remember ever feeling sad about many things other than a great memory. I believe in contentment and love and laughter. I believe when we fear for our content it is then, most of all, we feel sadness.

So tonight at around six o'clock I'll go with Eddie down by the river. We'll climb the fence and onto the pier off Jane Street and I hope that it will rain. I mean I hope it pours, pours down on us. I'll tell Blair in Farmville to stop her crying. Man, you know he's got nowhere to go but back to you. We'll talk of her and him and laugh and sing to the sweet melody of the Capris "There's a Moon Out Tonight." We'll leave it all up to Jackie Gleason to let us know when it's getting late. And right when Leonard's sun pours down like honey on our lady of the harbor, well it's then I'll look to the east and think of Father Angelo, I'll look to the west and think of Jimmy Mullen. I'll look north and south and think of all my angels, Indians, and saints that I've been so blessed to have come in contact with. I'll genuflect and thank my God, your God, our God, and as Mr. Ginsberg would say, "Tayatha Gate Gate Paragate Parasamgate Bodhi Svaha . . . on with the celebration."

And God saw the light, that it was good.
Gen. 1:4

211